Success Principles
UNLOCK YOUR LIMITLESS POTENTIAL

TEAGAN ADAMS

Copyright © 2018 Teagan Adams

All rights reserved.

ISBN-10: 1720462747

ISBN-13: 978-1720462743

TABLE OF CONTENTS

1	YOUR MINDSET IS YOUR BEST ASSET	Pg 1
2	RUN THE DAY OR THE DAY RUNS YOU	Pg 13
3	HARNESS THE LAW OF MOMENTUM	Pg 23
4	GREATNESS LIES OUTSIDE OF YOUR COMFORT ZONE	Pg 31
5	LAYOUT YOUR S.M.A.R.T. GOALS. THEN 10X THEM.	Pg 39
6	FORGET ABOUT WEAKNESSES. FOCUS ON STRENGTHS	Pg 48
7	MOTIVATION IS TEMPORARY, MOTIVE IS LASTING	Pg 55
8	NEVER, NEVER, NEVER GIVE UP	Pg 64
9	WITH A LEVER LONG ENOUGH YOU CAN MOVE THE WORLD	Pg 71
10	IF YOU ONLY FOCUS ON THE END RESULT YOU WILL LOSE	Pg 84
11	LAW OF ATTRACTION IS MEANINGLESS WITHOUT LAW OF ACTION	Pg 92

Teagan Adams

**Entrepreneurship 101 Course
(Valued at $97)**

FREE access at this link:
https://teagan.mykajabi.com/offers/gQzUPJ7A

In the Entrepreneurship 101 Course you will learn everything needed to start your own business, whether it be a side hustle on the side of school or a 9-5 job, or a full-time endeavor!

1 MINDSET IS YOUR BEST ASSET

The term 'placebo' has been used since the 1700's and was originally often a way to trick patients into thinking that they had been cured of some sort of ailment, when in reality they didn't actually have the proper medications to do so, and so the doctors would instead develop a fake pill called a placebo.

In 1996, fifty-six volunteers were involved in a study to test a new pain-killer called 'trivaricaine'. Each of the patients then had one of their index fingers covered in the new pain killer, while the other finger was left untouched. When the researchers pinched both of the patients' index fingers with a painful clamp, the patients came to the conclusion that the finger with this new pain-killer applied felt a lot less pain.

There was a catch though. This new pain-killer was actually just a random fake concoction with no pain easing properties at all. Although this fake substance didn't physically do anything at all to actually relieve the patients pain, they still did notice a substantial difference that was produced from the placebo cream giving its expected results. This cream didn't actually do anything, and yet to the patient, it actually did exactly what it was supposed to do.

The answer to this phenomenon lies in the power of your mind. All it takes is for you to believe something for your mind to be able to end up with the result that you were hoping for. When you truly believe that a pill, even if it is literally nothing, will actually help you, then when you take that pill you will actually trick your brain into believing that it is true, and then providing you with the desired result.

The mind is a powerful thing. When you need to overcome a certain ailment, even when it may seemingly need a much more sophisticated solution in the form of actual medications, in simply believing that you will be okay, your mind kicks in and makes that intangible thought into a tangible reality. The power of the mind is demonstrated in regards to medical outcomes and overcoming your physical ailments by simply believing that you can, but what if you could use this placebo effect to actually trick your brain into allowing you to achieve success in whatever it is that you are after?!

As I am sure you have already realized and probably already know, the mind is immensely powerful. The problem is that only 5% of your brainpower is used consciously, and the other 95% of your brainpower is all used up in your subconscious mind, and so if you are living reactively and only on the surface level rather than proactively going deeper and engaging your subconscious mind, then you are at a huge disadvantage. In order to be in the top 5% of people, you need to do what the other 95% aren't willing to do, and a great way to start with that is to leverage the 95% of your mind that is subconscious and proactively use that part of your mind to catapult your results.

I'm sure you have probably heard about how we only use a fraction of our brainpower, and how if you were to unlock the rest of your mind you would be able to do unfathomable things. You have probably seen movies like Limitless where they show the concept of what it could be like to be able to unlock more of your brain and in turn unlock your limitless potential.

Although I can't promise results like in those movies, what I can promise you is that if you are able to use what I am about to teach you to engage and harness your subconscious mind, you will see a substantial difference in your life.

Most of the time, you probably don't notice how your subconscious mind actually effects your thoughts and eventually your reality, and so you don't do anything to change it. The subconscious mind is super powerful, and you probably just don't really know it yet. When you go to bed at night, all throughout the night your subconscious mind is actually connecting the dots between things you experienced the day before, and connecting seemingly unrelated things, and so that is why the best time to be creative is right when you wake up, after your subconscious mind makes these connections, but more on that later. The thing that you need to understand though, is that you are likely wasting the power of your subconscious mind. If you go to bed straight away after consuming meaningless things like TV or video games, then that will be what your subconscious mind is focused on all throughout the night. And so instead of allowing yourself to fall into this state of reactivity where you allow your surroundings to dictate who you become, you need to learn to actually control your subconscious mind.

So how do you actually engage your subconscious mind and activate this placebo effect in relations to your life and overall success? The first thing that you need to understand is the Law of Attraction. The Law of Attraction is a belief that by focusing on the positive or negative aspects of life, they will bring positive or negative experiences and realities into their life. Through the Law of Attraction, you essentially have the power to transform your intangible thoughts into tangible outcomes, and the way to do so is through your subconscious mind.

I am sure that you have noticed a bit of a pattern all around you. The people that are struggling in life usually tend to get in a dangerous rut that causes a downward spiral that seems impossible to break free of. They start off in a bad situation, and this puts them in a negative mindset that then further brings in negative experiences into their life, making their circumstances worse, and in turn also making their mindset worse as well as they fall into an even more negative state of mind.

This situation seems hopeless, and I am sure that that is exactly how people in this situation feel, and that is exactly where the problem lies. When they just accept their fate and continue reacting to their negative circumstances and allowing those circumstances to drag them down with them, they are in fact hopeless. The thing that they need to realize though is that although their situation may be bad, they have the power to change it if they are willing.

Charles Swindoll once said that "Life is 10% what happens to you and 90% how you react to it". When people end up in this downward spiral, they allow themselves to become sucked in and they succumb to the reality that they think is just the way it is. But if they were able to just realize that they have the odds in their favor because 90% of life is how they react to their given circumstances, it would all be different. If instead of living reactively, they could turn the tables by simply reacting to their circumstances in a positive way and shifting their mindset towards the situation, they could alter their reality. Although they could be in a truly negative circumstance, the only way to break free from this downward spiral is to have a positive outlook towards the future.

Although the situation you could be in at this point in time could be negative and demanding, you get to choose you future. You have a choice to either succumb to the negative circumstances that you find yourself in, and allow those to shape your future, or instead of living reactively you can choose to proactively design the future that lies ahead of you.

I think that for the purpose of this book we should change the percentages in that quote to: "Life is 5% what happens to you and 95% how you react to it". As I mentioned earlier, your brain is 5% conscious and 95% subconscious, and so if you are only living on the surface level using only the 5% of your brain that is fully conscious and reactive to your negative surroundings, then you will continue down this negative spiral. But if you are able to proactively control your outlook towards a positive future, then you will be able to really dive deeper into a more subconscious level where you are able to control your subconscious emotions. And in doing so, in having a positive outlook towards your future, you will draw these positive opportunities and experiences into your life by harnessing the Law of Attraction, and ultimately turn your intangible thoughts and emotions into tangible outcomes.

So now you understand the story of those suffering with negativity that causes a downward spiral in their life, but would this given rule apply to those that seem to be on a continuous upward spiral? Would those people that we look up to, that seem to have it all, still follow this same set of rules, and could you say that their future was crafted proactively?

Some people might say that those people who are extremely successful in all aspects of life, who have truly unlocked their limitless potential, are all positive because their circumstances allow them to be. They get to live the life that most people only get to dream of living, and so it is no wonder that they have a positive outlook towards life. But I would argue that people who are successful aren't happy because of their success and the life that they get to live, but rather it is the other way around. The reason that they are successful and that they have unlocked their limitless potential is because they have always found a way to be positive, and therefore draw in positive opportunities for themselves. They are successful because of their positive outlook towards their life and life as a whole, which shapes their given reality.

Like I said earlier, the Law of Attraction takes your thoughts on the subconscious level, whether they be negative or positive, and provides your intangible thoughts and beliefs with their counterpart circumstances. The single greatest way to be successful and to unlock your limitless potential is not a product of luck or circumstance. You need to learn how to proactively craft and create your circumstances rather than allowing your circumstances to shape you. The first and greatest step towards success is to craft your outlook towards life in a positive way, to put yourself in a position to allow that positivity to reflect in your circumstances.

Your subconscious mind can't act on its own, and so you need to proactively suggest things to your subconscious mind through your consciousness. You need to consciously and consistently be planting the seeds into your subconscious mind in order to reap the results that you are looking for. You can think of your conscious mind as the gardener and you need to plant those seeds in the form of thoughts and ideas and emotions into your garden, being your subconscious mind. Once those seeds are planted, your subconscious mind will work day in and day out to provide the best soil for those seeds to grow, but only if you, the gardener, consciously tend to the garden by consistently reminding your subconscious mind of the soil that you are looking for, for your seeds of thought to grow in. If you are a surface level negative thinker, then that will translate into the soil to which your seeds are planted, and therefore you will end up with a terrible harvest. If you are optimistic however, you can produce the most beautiful garden, which will be your new circumstance that will then shoot your optimism up even higher and start this upward spiral towards your greater success. Be sure to use your conscious mind to plant flowers into your subconsciousness that will lead to your future happiness and ultimate success. Always tend to this garden, and don't let your mind be overcome with weeds.

Now that you understand that your beliefs shape your circumstances, as long as you live proactively, you have the power to craft your success. You need to shatter the extremely limiting belief that your current circumstances shape who you are, because if you allow that negativity to creep into your mindset, it will cause you to sink into that negative spiral. Think of it like quick sand – the more you struggle and try to resist it, and the longer you are in there, the harder it is to escape. So, act now, and act fast, and proactively create your perceived reality and have a positive outlook towards your future that will drive your success.

I want you to think for a second if you honestly think that you suck at drawing. If someone asked you to draw something, would your immediate response be something along the lines of "sure, but I suck at drawing"? If so, I would say that you are in the vast majority of people. And I bet that if you looked back to when you were a little kid, you would see that you actually weren't half bad at drawing, and it kind of looks like you gradually got worse.

Let me let you in on a little secret – You don't suck at drawing. I mean, maybe objectively you do, but on a deeper level, you don't have to suck at drawing. The reason that you suck at drawing is because you say so, and you really believe it, and so you are shaping your perceived reality in a negative way. When you were a little kid though, like most little kids you probably thought you were invincible, that you could do anything. And so naturally, you thought your drawings were next to Picasso and van Gogh. And because of this positive belief, your drawings probably weren't too bad. I mean, you still have to take into account that you were young, so naturally you weren't actually at Picasso's level, but they were still good.

Now that you are older though, you begin to doubt yourself. Limiting beliefs creep their way into your life and begin to cripple you. When you say that you are a bad drawer now, you are probably right. But you aren't saying that you are a bad drawer because you are a bad drawer. You are a bad drawer because you are saying that you are a bad drawer. Let that sink in. Your intangible thoughts create your tangible outcomes.

If you were able to tap in to that childlike invincibility, when you used to believe that you could do whatever you set your mind to, then you truly would be unstoppable. Imagine being able to combine your developed skills with a childlike positive self-outlook, and with the absence of limiting beliefs, then nothing would be able to stop you.

Albert Einstein, arguably the smartest man ever, says that he isn't actually smarter than anyone. In fact, he wasn't able to speak until he was four years old, and his teachers said that he "wouldn't amount to much". So already, you have an advantage over him because I'm sure that your teachers or past teachers would never say anything along the lines of that to you, and I am sure that you were quicker to learn how to speak that even Einstein. The reason though that Einstein says that people consider him to be so smart, and the reason that he had such huge breakthroughs, is not because of the circumstances or luck or God-given talents that shaped who he was. But rather, he actually proactively created his circumstances and ultimate success through one key thing: persistence. He actually said that "It's not that I am smarter, it's just that I stick with problems longer".

The reason that Albert Einstein became such a genius is because he didn't let his natural circumstances define or shape him. He could have just succumbed and accepted the fate that he was dumb. He was slower than the average kid in learning to talk, so right off the get-go he was below-average in terms of intellect. And all throughout school, he certainly wasn't the smartest kid, and teachers weren't afraid to point out the fact that he was 'dumb'. The average person, in his shoes, would have just accepted their reality and lived reactively and just allowed that to shape the person that they would become. If he had accepted this fate as his own, no one would have known his name. Instead, he was able to proactively create his future self. Instead of allowing his circumstances to shape who he was, he shaped his own circumstances through his persistence and his positive mindset.

His ability to not give up in the face of failure is the thing that ultimately set him up for future success. Instead of allowing his failures to send him into a downward spiral, he had his setbacks become the set-ups for his comebacks. He defined his future, and proactively created it through the power of his subconscious mind.

I think that the thing that made Albert Einstein a genius was not the fact that he was smart, but rather that he didn't give up, and that he instinctively knew that he could proactively create the reality that he desired by shifting his outlook towards life. Like I said already, you have an advantage over Albert Einstein, and you get to choose what you do with it. So rather than succumbing to the negatives that inevitably are around you in your life, you can choose today to define who you will become by planting that seed of optimism into your subconscious mind to reap those tangible outcomes that all spring from that single intangible idea.

The first principle of success is that you absolutely must think positively and have a positive outlook towards life if you want to attract positive opportunities and circumstances. If you believe that you can do whatever you set your mind to, then you will, because like Henry Ford said "Whether you think you can or you think you can't, you are right."

I actually leveraged this principle of success without even knowing it when I was a nine-year-old kid. I was just your average nine-year-old kid, but there was one main thing that set me apart, and that was my extremely positive mindset. I was only nine-years-old when I decided to audition to be on the national television show, Dragons Den. I had what was a pretty premature idea at the time, but I loved the show and so I thought it would be cool to audition, but I wouldn't allow myself to just stop there.

A few months went by after my initial audition and I still hadn't heard anything about me being on the show. At this point, most people would have just lost hope and moved on with their lives. That wasn't the case for me though. I still would talk about it almost every single day, talking like I had already made the show. I would say things like "Hey mom, when I go to Toronto to be on Dragons Den, will they pay for our flights or will you need to?" and "I'm excited to go on Dragons Den and meet the Dragons". I hadn't even gotten a call back, but I acted like I had already made the show, and I really believed it too.

In the end, I did end up getting that call back. I did end up flying to Toronto to pitch my idea (and yes, they did cover the travel expenses haha). I did end up meeting the Dragons. And I think the biggest thing that allowed me to actually accomplish this lies in the fact that instead of saying things like *if* I get chosen to go on Dragons Den, I said *when*. I believed that I could accomplish whatever I set my mind to, and I acted like I already had, and this positive mindset fueled my subconscious mind allowing my intangible thoughts to shape my tangible reality.

When I was on Dragons Den, I also didn't stop there. I allowed that to fuel my exponential growth. Instead of being happy with where I was and what I had accomplished, I started to proactively put myself in the position to get on that upward spiral.

The key is to get those successes early on so that they boost your mindset to an even more positive state of mind, and this causes that cycle where you get even a small win, celebrate it, and then allow that to fuel your positivity towards eventually accomplishing something even bigger, which makes you even more confident and positive. But as you are accomplishing these things, and celebrating them to allow that to fuel you, you cannot stay looking back. Like Babe Ruth said "yesterday's home runs don't win today's games".

You should be grateful and proud of all that you have accomplished and how far you've come, but don't let that be your downfall. You need to always be striving for more. Be grateful, but never be satisfied. Keep pushing yourself to new heights. Instead of looking back and admiring your successes in the past, you need to take action in the present, and allow your gratitude to fuel your flight to new heights.

Follow the wise words of Master Yoda, when he said "Do or do not, there is no try". You either do, or you don't do, but never say that you will try. You can do whatever set your mind to, so don't settle for 'trying' to do something. The first step towards unlocking your limitless potential lies in believing that you can do whatever you set your mind to, and you will.

2 RUN THE DAY OR THE DAY RUNS YOU

In this chapter, I want to teach you how you can prime yourself for success each and every day. Think of this chapter as a buffet – you can pick and choose what you would like to read and what you would like to apply into your own life. I would encourage you to read it all, and then afterwards pick what works for you. I don't want you to feel overwhelmed with all of the tactical strategies in this chapter to elevate your success on a daily basis, and so rather than feeling overwhelmed and not applying anything, I would encourage you to at least choose one thing and run with it. Like G.K. Chestersen said, "done is better than perfect". If your goal is perfection, you will never move forward and you will be stuck forever, but if you just take action and apply one thing, that will lead to many more things accomplished.

Even by just making your bed each morning, your life could be changed for the better. William McRaven wrote a book, Make Your Bed, and in that book, he says "If you make your bed every morning, you will have accomplished the first task of the day. It will give you a small sense of pride and it will encourage you to do another task and another and another. By the end of the day, that one task completed will have turned into many tasks completed.

Making your bed will also reinforce that the little things in life matter. If you can't do the little things right, you will never do the big things right".

This quote is a lot like what I was talking about in the previous chapter. When you celebrate the small wins, that helps you to become more positive and feel more competent, and that leads to you accomplishing more and getting into that upward spiral.

As I was saying, in this chapter I will be sharing with you lots of ways to level up your life and unlock your limitless potential by running each day proactively. I will be sharing with you lots of examples of things that have worked for other people, but they may not fit your lifestyle, so just choose at least one thing and run with it.

In the last chapter, I touched on the idea of causing your subconscious mind to work for you throughout the night by priming it before you go to bed, rather than falling victim to consuming things like social media or TV or video games right before you go to bed, because it would be a huge waste to have your subconscious mind all throughout the night connecting things from those. Instead, you should prime your subconscious before you go to bed, so that all throughout the night it will be working on connecting between things and ideas that you came across to come across meaningful ideas and conclusions relating to your greater goals.

Thomas Edison said to "never go to sleep without a request to your subconscious". Thomas Edison was an extremely successful man, and he says that a great amount of that success stems from the fact that he was able to use his subconscious to lead him to valuable conclusions and connecting seemingly unrelated things to come up with great ideas.

A successful day starts the night before, with a good night's sleep so you can have energy for the next day, and with your subconscious mind working double time to connect the dots and allow you to come to valuable conclusions.

The next part to this is that the first few hours of your day are the most important. They determine either the success or failure of the day to come. The way to achieve success and an extraordinary life, is to do extraordinary things each and every day. If you wake up and immediately fall victim to the distractions of everyday life, and you allow yourself to go throughout your day being reactive to your surroundings with all of the notifications going on around you, then you will be a lot less likely to live extraordinarily each day because you will fall into the mold of society and you will end up just going through the motions.

The way to be successful is to break free from this mold, and the way to do so is to start your day in a meaningful and proactive way so that you can set yourself up for success that day, ultimately leading to greater success. If you are able to run the day rather than letting the day run you, then you can break free from this mold of society and unlock your limitless potential.

David Bednar said "In my office is a beautiful painting of a wheat field. The painting is a vast collection of individual brushstrokes— none of which in isolation is very interesting or impressive. In fact, if you stand close to the canvas, all you can see is a mass of seemingly unrelated and unattractive streaks of yellow and gold and brown paint. However, as you gradually move away from the canvas, all of the individual brushstrokes combine together and produce a magnificent landscape of a wheat field. Many ordinary, individual brushstrokes work together to create a captivating and beautiful painting."

This painting is a great analogy for our life. Each day we can easily think that it doesn't really matter if we really live proactively, because there is always tomorrow, and I mean what's one day? But the only way to be successful in the long term is to build up consistency on a daily basis. You need to develop positive habits and routines that allow you to live proactively and eventually stretch yourself towards greatness. Although each day may seem like just one individual brushstroke, if you look at the grander vision of what you could accomplish in the bigger picture by consistently focusing each day, you can understand why each day matters.

The single most important way to run the day before the day runs you is to start each morning the right way, and that starts the night before with your request to your subconscious. After your subconscious mind has now been connecting thoughts and ideas, you need to find a way to bring those thoughts and ideas to your conscious mind, and a great way to do that is to start off by journaling first thing in the morning.

When I say journaling, I don't mean the kind where you write all of the gossip going on in your life, or about that guy or girl that you have a crush on. The kind of journaling that I am talking about is much deeper and a lot more meaningful.

What you should really be doing in your journal is just writing out all of your thoughts and ideas, your dreams and aspirations. Just get it all down on paper and do what is called a brain dump. Just get it all out there and see where things connect. Pretty soon, you will see connections that you didn't notice before and everything will start connecting and flowing and you get in a peak state. You should also write out your big goals each morning to keep those at the top of your mind and allow them to be your guiding paradigm of your life that you can then base your day to day decisions and actions on. If you don't have a big goal that drives you, and if you don't remind yourself of that goal consistently, then you will find yourself just drifting through life. What you need to do is set a clear goal and keep it at the top of your mind, so that you can start taking specific steps in the right direction, rather than just wandering aimlessly through life.

Another important part of this brain dump revolves around what is known as your working memory. Your working memory is basically just your short-term memory, the things that are on your mind right now, and for most people it can cripple their success and stunt their growth.

Doing a brain dump is important for right when you wake up to reflect on your subconscious mind's connections, and to prime yourself for the day ahead of you, but it is also important to do the night before as well. Before you prime your subconscious, you should have a brain dump in your journal where you just get all of your ideas and thoughts, and really anything that is on your mind down on paper. On top of this, you should also write down what you have planned for tomorrow and lay out your goals for the next day to set yourself up for success.

The reason that you should do these brain dumps revolves around your working memory. Your working memory is defined as being a "a system for temporarily storing and managing the information required to carry out complex cognitive tasks such as learning, reasoning, and comprehension". You working memory stores all of your current thoughts and ideas of what is going on right now in the present moment.

The problem with your working memory is that it can cause you to not be thinking creatively, and it can cause you to blindly miss out on ideas and opportunities that are right in front of you. Allow me to explain.

Often times we have so many ideas floating around in our heads, as well as lots of things that you are trying to remember to do for later on in the day or the week, and so you fill up your brain with these things that you need to do, and that leaves little to no room for new ideas to happen. You crowd out the creativity from your mind and instead solely focus on the things that are right in front of you, which is again another way of living reactively.

The way to get creative ideas is often not even when you are in the middle of working on something, but rather when you disconnect and take the time to rest and reset, because this disconnection allows your subconscious to come in and make connections with the words around you and subconsciously connect the dots leading to new and creative ideas. But when you fill your working memory, your conscious mind, with meaningless tasks and to-dos, it doesn't allow your subconscious mind to fully activate and engage and come up with new ideas, and so you stunt your growth by living reactively.

The way to overcome this is by writing down your ideas. It is so simple, and yet extremely effective, and it is a strategy that so many of the most successful people swear by. If you are able to either write down your ideas and tasks and things that you need to do in the notes on your phone, then it allows your mind to be free of that so it has space to come up with new ideas. Or another option is to just do things right away as they come to your mind to get it done with and out of your mind, but this isn't always the best strategy because although you may think you can, you definitely cannot actually multitask effectively. When you are constantly switching from one task to another, you waste a lot of time because of the time it takes to transition and to refocus. So instead of this, you should batch your time and schedule focus blocks to get a lot more done, a lot faster, but more on that in the chapter on the Law of Momentum.

Now that you understand why your working memory can cripple your growth, you probably can guess why it is important to do a brain dump before you go to bed. You need to get this meaningless dead weight out of your working memory so that you can allow your subconscious to work extra hard on connecting the dots and connecting ideas all throughout the night. So, before you go to bed, first of all do a brain dump and get all of your thoughts and ideas and tasks and to-dos onto paper and plan out the goals you have for tomorrow. Then make sure to proactively have a request to your subconscious, by priming your mind with meaningful things relating to your greater goals. Then right when you wake up, record your ideas once more from the connections that were made by your subconscious mind while you were asleep.

The next couple of hours are vitally important, and this is the time where you will be the most effective and creative. Even if you consider yourself to not at all be an early-bird, you need to be. Almost all successful people beat the sun up each morning, and there is a science-backed reasoning behind this.

The first few hours of your day are vitally important because of how they position the rest of your day to either be successful or a complete waste of time, but also because in these first few hours you are a lot more creative and after sleeping your brain, especially your prefrontal cortex, is firing much faster, and is more effective and creative, and you will also have all of the connections from your subconscious from the night before that could lead to ground-breaking ideas.

You need to take advantage of this peak state that can happen each morning, and it is worth it to go to bed earlier if you have to so that you can wake up a couple of hours earlier than you usually do so that you can start your day off right, instead of just waking up and going through the motions of getting ready for school or work and then just living reactively for the rest of your day.

Most people just wake up and grab their phones and fall victim to the system. You can leverage this age of distractedness by being focused and proactive, which are actually much more important than pure talent these days. If you are able to be the person that takes that step to actually live proactively and set themselves up for success each morning, then you will stand out from the crowd and unlock your limitless potential.

If you are able to actually wake up early and get your number one priority done right away, or the one that needs the most creativity, then you will have a huge jump on your day, and this will start the chain reaction that will lead to you accomplishing a lot more in the rest of your day, and ultimately a lot more in life. You will get a huge head start on everyone else, and you will be able to live much more proactively and achieve whatever you set your mind to.

Another way to run the day is to generate energy. Energy is extremely important, and it will allow you to accomplish your goals much more effectively and be a lot more productive throughout your day. The first thing that you need to understand about energy is that we are like powerplants. We don't *have* energy. We need to generate it. I will be sharing with you a few useful ways that you can generate the energy necessary to successfully run the day.

The first thing that you should do is exercise. Exercise is extremely important, because you are the vehicle that will drive you to your success. When Confucius said that "The man who chases two rabbits catches none", he didn't mean that you should go all in on your business or your passion and neglect things like your health, but a lot of people think that that is what you need to do. If only they understood that if they took the time each day to actually get the right amount of exercise, they would end up saving a lot of time because when they do get to working they will be a lot more effective. And on top of that, a study also found that consistent exercise can slow down aging by as much as ten years! So that time it takes to exercise each day is a small price to pay for more energy, more productivity, and up to ten more years of living!

Another powerful way to increase your energy and make you much more productive and effective is to take cold showers. I know, it doesn't sound very appealing but it does work. In fact, there was a study with a group of people who were asked to take cold showers for a couple of weeks and see how they felt. In the end, although almost all of them didn't want to have cold showers, most of them ended up sticking with the routine because they noticed the difference it had on their life. Not only does having a cold shower give you an adrenaline rush that spikes your energy, but it also has long-term benefits such as treating depression symptoms because the cold water triggers a wave of mood boosting chemicals that make you happier. It also boosts your metabolism which helps you to be able to lose weight, and it has positive benefits around your immune, lymphatic, circulatory, and digestive systems. Overall, it not only wakes you up and generates energy on a day to day basis, but it also has long-term benefits that can improve your overall quality of life.

Whatever you do, just do something. Do your best to live each day proactively and build up consistency on a daily basis. Never go to sleep without a request to your subconscious and allow your subconscious mind to come to creative conclusions by freeing up space in your working memory so that you can focus on the present moment and have creative breakthroughs. Wake up early to get a jump on the day and do the little things like making your bed that start that chain reaction towards eventually accomplishing your greater goals. Leverage those first few hours to use the connections that were made from your subconscious mind loosely wandering and connecting the dots while you slept and get those creative breakthroughs right away so you can start each day by living proactively. Whatever you do, just make sure that you don't fall victim to reactivity by designing your life the way you want it.

3 HARNESS THE LAW OF MOMENTUM

Newton's first law of motion states that objects in motion tend to stay in motion, and objects at rest tend to stay at rest. This law of motion applies to us as well, in the form of productivity. The problem with it though, is that many people are in the second scenario – an object at rest tends to stay at rest. This is the case of procrastination. When you don't take action and you fall victim to the distractions of everyday life you start to get sucked deeper and deeper. An object in rest tends to stay in rest. Like I talked about in the last chapter, if you start your day off by reacting to your environment, that will likely be the determinant of the day ahead. If right when you wake up you immediately check your phone and fall victim to life's distractions, then that will likely cause you to stay in a state of reactivity and procrastination for the rest of your day. It's like when you sit and watch a movie for a couple of hours in the middle of the day and then afterwards you just don't feel like doing anything at all, so when you get home you drop back onto the couch. An object at rest tends to stay at rest.

Although this law of motion can be a killer of productivity in that people procrastinate and then that leads to them procrastinating even further, it doesn't have to be that way. There are two sides to this equation, and the key to beating procrastination is on the other side of this equation. If you want to beat procrastination and gain massive momentum in your life, then you need to take a look at the other part of Newton's first law of motion.

An object in motion tends to stay in motion. If you are able to understand this law of motion, it can help you to understand how easy it really is to get things done and overcome procrastination. We live in the information age, with limitless information readily available, right at our fingertips, but the problem with this information overload is that it can easily lead to us feeling overwhelmed and not having any idea where to even begin, and so procrastination takes over. The way to defeat analysis paralysis is to harness this principle of momentum by first of all stopping overthinking things, and then just taking action.

The first step to gaining momentum is to just start. Think about the last time you had to do some sort of writing assignment. It probably started off with you staring at that super annoying blinking cursor for a little while, not even knowing where to begin. But then once you realize that you actually really need to get this done as soon as possible, then panic kicks in and so you just start and write your first sentence. And then all of a sudden, another idea comes to you and other, and another. The ideas and concepts just start flooding in and everything starts connecting, and before you know it you have a finished product.

If you feel stuck, a great way to overcome this is to just start. Gil Penchina said that "momentum begets momentum, and the best way to start is to start". If you don't know where to even start, then just start. I know this sounds super counterintuitive but if you feel like you don't know where to even begin on something, the best way to find your way is to just start. If you are supposed to write an essay but you are experiencing major writer's block, then maybe you could just write down the title and get your name and date down and write the first sentence about what you will be talking about and before you know it the words will just keep flowing. The act of just starting can help you to be able to gain momentum, and honestly just getting started is the hardest part of almost any task, and once you do it, that is half of the work done right there.

One of the biggest things that stops people from taking action and ultimately prevents them from unlocking their limitless potential is being a perfectionist. I mentioned this quote by G.K. Chestersen earlier, but it is definitely worth repeating. He said that "done is better than perfect". If you focus on waiting until you have the perfect final product of something, or you wait for the perfect timing, then you will never start, and you will never gain momentum, and ultimately you will never succeed. You need to understand that the timing will never be right, and you can't let that stop you. If you want to be a YouTuber, don't wait until you can save up for a nice camera and full-blown set up. Just start recording on your phone and improve as you go. There are plenty of viral videos out there today that were filmed on phones. You can never know if that one video that you wanted to film would have gone viral or not, and if it really was a funny or valuable or moving video, then it is completely irrelevant if the quality isn't top-tier. Just start, and improve as you go, because like Picasso said "only put off until tomorrow what you would be willing to die having left undone".

Now I want you to think of a recent assignment or some sort of something that you needed to do by a certain time. You wouldn't be unusual if you waited until the last minute to even start on getting that done. I bet this is a familiar story to you: You get assigned to do something, and you fully intend to get started right away and chip away at it over time, but sure enough time slips by and the due date is tomorrow. You sit down and get absolutely focused and whip something up. Not that I am pro-procrastination or anything, but you can likely produce much better quality of work than if you had chopped up your work, while also saving a lot of time. When you just sit down and get started and then stick to something for a long period of time and you have absolute isolated focus, you are able to gain so much momentum and it gets to the point where the ideas and concepts just start flooding in and everything starts connecting. The non-procrastinator never gets in the zone like this and is a lot less effective because of the time it takes to transition and refocus.

Don't get me wrong though, I am not vouching for procrastination or anything, but rather my point is that you can gain a lot of momentum when you focus for a long period of time with no distractions and get extremely focused on what you are doing. I bet you think you are a professional multitasker. You think you can save so much time when you go crazy and do tons of things all at once, constantly shifting from one task to another. I hate to tell you this, but you actually can't multitask. It is proven that when you try multitasking, your intellect drops to approximately that of an eight-year-old because you aren't focusing on just one thing. So yes, when people are texting while driving, they not only have their eyes off the road, but they also drop to the intellect of eight-year-olds.

My point with all of this is that there is a difference between being busy and being productive. It may seem like when you are madly dashing from one task to the next that you are getting a lot done, but you are actually wasting a lot of time because of the time it takes to transition and refocus. Imagine for a second that you have a car that you have to push all the way from point A to point B. The example of the person that is absolutely focused on one thing would take that car and push, struggling at first, but eventually it starts rolling and it gets to the point where they don't even need to do anything. They just let momentum do its job. The person that is multitasking on the other hand would push that car for a little bit, and then just as it starts moving they switch to something else. When they then switch back to the car, they have to start from square one again.

You can't multitask, and no you are not the one exception. Face it, that is exactly what every single one of us says. If you are able to accept this and instead of being 'busy' if you were to work harder, you could gain momentum and nothing would be able to stop you. And this is actually backed by science. When you strategically structure your time to proactively craft your schedule so that you can have focus blocks with zero distraction, a white tissue called myelin develops over your neurons. Myelin actually makes your brain cells fire much faster, thus making you much more effective and creative. You get so focused that the ideas are just flooding in faster than you can catch them and everything is connecting.

One of the first people to talk about this idea of getting in the zone was Mihaly Csikszentmihalyi. He coined the term of 'flow states', which is something relating to gaining momentum that is extremely powerful and can help you to not only work more productively and creatively, but also feel much more fulfilled and happy and present in what it is that you are doing.

Mihaly Csikszentmihalyi says that "when you are in a flow state, every action, every movement and thought follows inevitably from the previous one", which is a lot like what I was just talking about. When you get in a state of flow, the ideas just keep flooding in, connecting from one idea to the next. You become in a peak state of ultimate brainpower and creativity. When in a state of flow, you can really unlock your limitless potential. The question is, how can you create these experiences? How can you make yourself go into a state of flow? And how can you do so every day so that you can truly unlock your limitless potential?! To find out, let's dig a little deeper and go into the origin of flow-states.

Mihaly Csikszentmihalyi originally coined the term of flow states in 1975. It started with research around top performers, especially in industries such as professional athletics as well as freestyle rappers. There was a study done to figure out how they put themselves in a pique state so that they can perform at such high levels. He found that high performers, from athletes to musicians, said that when they were performing or competing, they would be so fully immersed in what they were doing that they essentially lose all sense of space and time. They lose all emotional baggage because they are absolutely 100% immersed in the present moment, and that is why it is such a great feeling. And by the way, when Mihaly Csikszentmihalyi started his study, it originally began as a search for happiness. It appears that he found it in the form of these flow states, because when in one you are completely at peace with no negative emotions dragging you down. And as a bonus, and the main reason that we are after these pique states, is that when in a flow state you are so much more creative and ideas just keep flooding in and you can work extremely productively, so whether you want to be a musician, athlete, entrepreneur, or anything under the sun, you can leverage flow states to gain massive momentum and unlock your limitless potential.

The way to access a state of flow, is to first of all, figure out what it is that puts you in that state of flow. It needs to be something that you absolutely love to do, and maybe you can think of a time when you were doing that thing and you lost sense of space and time because you were fully engaged. That would be a great start. Once you have an idea of what that thing is, you need to increase two key things around it, and find the sweet spot between the two, which is where a state of flow is waiting for you. These two things are skill, and challenge. If you have no skill in a certain thing, and you aren't being challenged by it, then you will feel apathetic towards it. This is the opposite of a state of flow. If you were extremely skilled at something but you aren't being challenged by it, then that won't lead to a state of flow either, but rather a state of boredom. If you are feeling challenged by it but you are lacking the necessary skills, then that will lead to anxiety, not a state of flow. So, you need to combine the two, by both challenging yourself, and having adequate skills enough to meet that challenge whilst stretching yourself, then that is when you have found your flow state. And when you work towards overcoming that challenge, although it will be challenging and it will stretch you, when you are in a state of flow it will seem effortless, and that is exactly how you can unlock your limitless potential.

Remember though that the first step towards gaining momentum and getting in a state of flow lies solely in just getting started. Once you take that first step, you shift from a state of rest to a state of motion. You break free from being an object in rest that stays in rest, and instead you are able to leverage the law of motion that states that an object in motion stays in motion. Now that you are in motion, continue gaining momentum by structuring your time so that you can work with time rather than against it, because yes time does fly, but you are the pilot. If you can structure your time into focused blocks of absolute isolated focus then you will gain momentum and get ahead while being a lot more effective and creative. And the best way to get in a state of flow is when you have these isolated focused blocks of time which cause you to get absolutely in the zone, which is a state of flow. In the next chapter, I will expand more on what I was talking about when I said how in order to reach a state of flow, you need to challenge yourself, because the next chapter is based around the principle that greatness lies outside of your comfort zone.

4 GREATNESS LIES OUTSIDE OF YOUR COMFORT ZONE

In the last chapter, I talked a little bit about how not feeling challenged by something makes you feel bored, and on the flipside how when something is too challenging and you don't have the necessary skill to match that challenge, it leads to anxiety. But you do need challenge in your life, you just need the proper amount that will allow you to grow and stretch yourself and your abilities without causing you to feel so overwhelmed that you quit.

Michael Hyatt said that "When it comes to meaningful achievement, comfort equals boredom and low engagement". When you get comfortable in life, not only do you plateau and remain average, but you also won't feel engaged in life and you won't feel fulfilled. This is exactly why you see people like Warren Buffett, who at the age of eighty-seven is still working away, even though his net worth is estimated to be around $83,000,000,000. Clearly, he doesn't have any need to keep working. Most people would retire a couple of decades before him, with only a small fraction of the money that he has. The reason that he keeps working though is because it keeps him feeling fulfilled, and thus feeling happy. He likes the way that he is always stretched and even at his level he is still consistently stretched to grow and become better than he was yesterday. He still gets outside of his comfort zone, and it has allowed him to live a much more meaningful life.

Generally, people equate comfort with happiness. We assume that living a life completely comfortably would make us happy. If only we could quit our jobs or leave school and just spend each day living in a mansion with a pool and a full theatre and an oceanfront view and seven Ferrari's, one for each day of the week, then we would be happy. I am willing to bet that although this does sound super appealing, if you actually had that as your reality, you would very quickly lose interest and you would begin to feel lost and unfulfilled. I think that a much better life would be starting out below average in terms of wealth but having those big ambitions to one day earn your way to the top, and then it is that journey that is the awesome part. When you love the journey and embrace that discomfort, it allows you to level up as a person and become who you need to be to succeed. Personally, I would much rather have the second option be my reality. I would rather start from the bottom but with the right mindset and drive and determination, than start at the top and live a meaningless life.

The reason that so many successful people don't just stop working when they reach the heights of heights is because they learned to love the struggle. They love the stress and the constant pressure to become better than they were yesterday. It fuels them and they love it. It is exhilarating. They start from the bottom with big ambitions, only to find that when they finally reach the top, the thing that really makes them happy is the fulfillment that comes from the struggle.

The only way to be successful is to embrace discomfort. You must embrace this struggle. Whether you like it or not, you must tackle it head on, and I assure you that you will learn to find the comfort in being uncomfortable which will drive you to the highest of heights.

Surfers can be great examples of embracing discomfort, especially those surfers that surf those huge waves. When you are riding one of these enormous waves, you have no choice than to successfully ride the wave. If you fall, you will be crushed and have a pretty high chance of dying. They don't succumb to the pressure though. They feel the pressure, and they understand the dangers, but they embrace this discomfort. Instead of allowing it to make them choke up and fall, they allow the pressure to make them perform at their absolute highest levels, to be able to accomplish this menacing task. They use their discomfort to make success necessary. It is literally life or death, succeed or die.

Instead of allowing the discomfort of a given situation to overwhelm you, you should allow it to keep you on edge enough that you know it is there, but then allow that to make you perform better. The adrenaline sets in and you become unstoppable. This is how you get in the flow state like we talked about earlier. You need to challenge yourself and allow that challenge, that discomfort, to allow you to need to perform at your highest abilities, and so this state of flow kicks in.

Another example of embracing discomfort is one of my own. I was trying to learn to do a front flip on my friend's trampoline, and I had finally figured out the basics of what I needed to do, but each time when I felt ready to try and land the front flip, I would do the same thing over and over again. I would jump for a little while, getting as high as I could so that I would have plenty of air time to be able to do the full rotation and hopefully land on my feet. But then every single time, I would jump up into the air, wait until I hit the trampoline to bounce up once more, and then just as I lifted off I would go. I wouldn't even allow myself to reach the height that I needed to in order to do the full rotation, and so every time I would flip too early, and since I wasn't nearly high enough above the trampoline, I would end up landing on my neck. As much as it hurt to land on my neck time and time again, I was still too scared to jump at the top of my bounce. I felt like when I was up in the air I would be too high and I would be more likely to get hurt, because if I fell on my head it would really hurt. But I was actually sabotaging myself because I wanted to stay inside my comfort zone, where I thought it was safe, when I would do the small bounce and constantly land on my neck. When I finally decided to actually go at the top of my bounce and get outside of my comfort zone, I immediately did the full rotation and landed perfectly on my feet. Sometimes your comfort zone isn't actually the safest place to be, and you can self-sabotage yourself by relying on your comfort zone too heavily.

Sometimes certain things can seem scarier, but in reality, they are actually a much safer option. Although you may need to stretch outside of your comfort zone, you could be going into territories that in reality are much safer. People as a whole are generally much more scared of riding in airplanes than they are in cars, but I bet you didn't know that the chances of your dying in a plane crash are one in a million. The chances of you dying in a car crash on the other hand are one in five-thousand. Planes are generally scarier to most people because of how high you are, so if you were to crash it would be pretty unlikely that you would survive. In a car on the other hand, you generally feel safe and secure, but in reality, you are much more likely to die of a car crash. Sometimes the safer bet lies outside of your comfort zone. When setting goals, you are actually scientifically proven to be more likely to accomplish your goals the bigger they are. Although setting huge goals that seem impossible may be outside of your comfort zone, you will be more likely to accomplish those big goals than some mediocre ones because they motivate and drive you to be passionate and get creative in figuring out how to accomplish those goals, but more on that in the next chapter. Setting big goals that are outside of your comfort zone gets you super engaged and focused and makes your life feel more meaningful, and makes you feel much more fulfilled.

Kyle Maynard is the perfect example of someone who lives life outside of their comfort zone. Although he was born with no arms or legs, he has wrestled for one of the best teams of Southeast America, he holds records in weightlifting, he has fought mixed martial arts, and he also crawled all the way to the summit of Mt Kilimanjaro, the largest mountain in Africa. Instead of just living in the comfort of his home, assuming that life gave him a disadvantage, he set out for greatness. He got outside of his comfort zone and crushed his goals. Not only did he get outside of his comfort zone of doing things like climbing Mt Kilimanjaro with no arms or legs, but he also did what would be outside of people's comfort zones who did have arms and legs. And yet the average person would likely let that discomfort zone keep them caged. Kyle Maynard was able to break free from this cage, and he has accomplished way more in his thirty-two years than most people do in a life time, and he did it all with no arms and no legs. What's your excuse?

One way that people are often put outside of their comfort zones in a way that enables them to grow is in learning to swim. The only way to swim is to just jump into that discomfort and force yourself to stay above the water. Usually it is a bit more of a process than that for the average person, starting with a life jacket and their parents help, eventually working their way up to water wings and then nothing but their parents help and then finally with the close watch of their parents, they try swimming on their own. This extensive process wasn't the case for Kyle Maynard. Instead, his dad just put him straight into the deep end, and even without arms of legs, he was able to learn how to swim. This place outside of his comfort zone allowed him to grow and learn that he could overcome his challenge and do whatever he set his mind to.

When you are getting outside of your comfort zone, you also have to come at challenges with a growth mindset, where you either win or you learn. If you understand this, then you will be invincible. Sure, you will fail. A lot. But those failures will only set you up for future success, and they will shape you into the person that deserves that success.

Earlier I talked about the role of both the subconscious and the conscious mind. They affect you in terms of your comfort zone as well. When you are trying something new or stretching beyond your current conscious abilities, your subconscious mind kicks in and makes you feel fear or anxiety. It is wired to keep you within your comfort zone as an age-old survival mechanism, but in this case all it is doing is preventing you from growing as a person. When you feel this fear and anxiety when you are trying to accomplish something, it is a sign that you are on the right track because you can tell that you are beginning to get outside of your comfort zone, which is the only way that you are able to grow.

Whether you used to be in school, or still are, you know the feeling when you start a new grade in math and it seems like a whole new thing. But you obviously don't let that stop you from carrying on. Although you may feel fear and anxiety, you keep moving forward because you know you need to. And because of this, you allow this to become your new comfort zone. When you get outside of your comfort zone, you stretch yourself as a person so that you can grow and level up, but you also actually stretch the point where your comfort zone lies. When you finally figure out this new grade level of math, it because your new level, and sure enough the next challenge lies ahead of you. If you could look at your life the same way as you did with school, as a requirement to get outside of your comfort zone by learning the next step and growing as a person and stretching your comfort zone, then you would unlock your limitless potential.

Carol Dweck is the person that originally brought about the idea of the growth mindset, which has been popularized a lot since then. There are two core types of mindsets that seperate the people that succeed in life from the people that remain average. These two mindsets are known as the growth mindset and the fixed mindset. Before I go on to explaining what each of these is, I want you to answer this question in your head: Do you believe that you can become smarter, or is your intellect fixed? If you said no, that you cannot become smarter than you are today, then I hate to tell you but you have a fixed mindset, and that is likely the thing that is keeping you captive to your limiting beliefs and preventing you from unlocking your limitless potential. Don't worry though, you can still develop a growth mindset that will allow you to unlock your limitless potential, because all it is really is just a simple belief.

People with a fixed mindset believe that their fate is set and that they can't do anything about it. They believe that they can't control their circumstances, even though we shattered this limiting belief in the first chapter. They think that they can't improve, and so they don't. People with a growth mindset on the other hand are always up for a challenge. Instead of feeling upset if they can't figure something out at first, they don't give up and assume that they aren't good enough, but rather they take it as an opportunity to learn and grow. They know that their mindset and even who they are as a person is fluid. They can change if they want to, and they can do so for the better. And since people with a growth mindset believe this and they believe that they either win and succeed or they learn and grow, it allows them to get outside of their comfort zone consistently. With the understanding that they cannot truly fail, and that when they mess up they are just one step closer to victory, they are able to stretch themselves outside of their comfort zones, leading up to unlocking their limitless potential and achieving greater success.

Even if you think you have a fixed mindset now, you need to understand that that isn't your set reality. Your set reality is fluid as long as you believe it is. All it takes is a small shift in your mindset towards believing that you can grow in every way to set yourself up for success. If you believe that you can grow, and you take challenges as opportunities to do so, then you will be invincible.

5 SET YOUR S.M.A.R.T. GOALS. THEN 10X THEM

I am sure that you have been told over and over again to set 'S.M.A.R.T.' goals. If you ask me, I would say that S.M.A.R.T. goals are just plain dumb. Part of the formula for setting S.M.A.R.T. goals is correct, such as keeping your goals specific and measurable and time-limited. But saying that you should keep your goals realistic and attainable is a complete lie. You should NEVER keep your goals attainable. If you are setting goals that seem possible then you are doing something wrong. You need to set your goals so big that they get you out of bed each morning with the drive and determination to get to work. Your goals should be so big so that rather than you having to push yourself to work towards your goals, you can just let the gravitational field of that monumental goal pull you straight to it.

A great indicator that you are doing something right is when people think you are crazy. Naveen Jain said that you should "think so big, so audaciously that people think you are crazy". All great ideas were once considered to be crazy. If your ideas and goals seem crazy to average minded people then you know that you are on the right track to unlocking your limitless potential. Daniel Burnham said "Make no little plans. They have no magic to stir men's blood and probably will not themselves be realized. Make big plans, aim high in hope and work". Don't set small goals, because they will likely not be realized. When you set small goals, they don't motivate you and get you excited and so you aren't nearly as engaged. I think you would be much more likely to accomplish a goal to start a business and make $1,000 in the first month than you would be to make $100, because that gets you a lot more motivated. Maybe $100 seems like a lot for you, and if so then that could be a good place to start, or maybe $1,000 doesn't seem very challenging, so shoot for $10,000. It's all about being self-aware and understanding your circumstances and looking through your own perspective.

You need to understand that you can accomplish whatever you set your mind to, and so you may as well aim high. If you knew that you would be guaranteed to make at least $1 million this year if you set that goal, then would you do it? The thing is, you can. If you actually believe you can and then take action on it and put in the work necessary, then you can do whatever you set your mind to. And of course, we all have different circumstances, so maybe you don't need to shoot that high, but why not? Shoot for the moon and even if you don't quite make it, you will land among the stars.

Russell Brunson, founder of ClickFunnels, was once into wrestling. He had his own team in his hometown of Boise, Idaho, and he was super passionate about the sport. One day his dad took him to a state wrestling match. He was super intrigued, and this lit a fire within him to one day wrestle in the state championships himself. This was a big goal to him, and he knew that he could accomplish it, so he got to work, and sure enough he ended up wrestling in the state championships. He was extremely proud of what he was able to have accomplished by setting the bar high and going for that big goal. But then he found out that one of his fellow wrestlers that he knew had recently been to a national wrestling championship. Like Russell Brunson, he was inspired and he set a goal and aimed high, but instead of aiming for the state championships like Russell, he decided that he would one day wrestle at the national level. And he did. Although him and Russell Brunson were both around the same skill level, the only thing that set them apart was that one of them decided to set his goal higher. They both set goals, and they both accomplished their goals, but in reality, Russell Brunson could have gone much higher, and all he needed to do in order to get there was to aim higher. Let this be a lesson to you to set your goals high, and once you think you've set your goals at a nearly impossible place, go even higher.

I bet you didn't know that a domino can knock over another domino being 50% larger. So eventually by the 23rd domino you would be able to knock over the next domino being the size of the Eiffel tower, and by the 57th domino you would be able to knock over the next domino being tall enough to reach the moon. So, starting with that little two-inch block, you can eventually knock over huge things. This domino effect applies to us and our lives as well because we can set our goals high, but in order to get there we also need to start today on the task that is right in front of us. Set your goals, and shoot for the moon, but then start today on the task that is right in front of you. Although I have been encouraging you to set your goals extremely high, you also need to remember to actually take action. Although it is important to visualize and get excited about those greater goals, you also need to take action today by laying out the foundation to eventually work your way up to accomplishing those huge goals.

A lot of people are living life in the middle, but the way to succeed and crush your goals is to live in the extremes. An example of living in the extremes is in what Gary Vaynerchuk calls the clouds and the dirt. The clouds being your overall mindset, your mission, your greater why (something that we will be talking about later on), and your ultimate goals. The dirt being the execution, the work that has to be put in to create the diamonds that we all strive for. You should only focus on the overall philosophy being the clouds, and the details, being the dirt, and nothing in the middle

You need to have the clouds as a grander vision to guide you so that you know where you are going so that you can take strategic steps in that direction, and you need that ultimate goal to drive you. But then you need to not waste all of your time in the planning stages and in laying out the greater vision and philosophy. You need to face the fact that excessive planning is really just fancy procrastination. You need to lay out your ultimate goals and your greater vision and allow that to guide your day to day decisions because you need a clear direction of where to go or else you will inevitably start wandering and get lost. But then once you have those clouds laid out, it is now time to spend a lot of time in the dirt to eventually work your way towards that greater vision. And some aspects of the dirt aren't going to be fun. I mean who likes dirt? But as long as you have that greater vision at the top of your mind, you will know why you are doing this, and it will fuel you. And along the way, you will also probably learn to genuinely love the dirt. Most successful people will say that they have learned to love the work. Like I talked about earlier, they love the journey and they love to always be challenging themselves to grow as a person.

As I said, you need to set specific goals so that you can understand exactly where you are going and then go straight to that destination. If you don't have a clear goal then you will end up aimlessly wandering through life like most people, and so you won't gain very much distance towards any given direction. You need to have a clear goal and have laser vision towards accomplishing that goal. But still don't worry about wavering a little bit on the way to accomplishing that grander vision. The goal should never change, but the plan that leads you there can and should have a little leniency. As long as you stick to your end-goal, you should never become discouraged if you have a short-term loss. Some parts of your plan may not work out, and that is not a fail. What would be a fail is if you become discouraged and give up because of that short-term loss. These short-term losses actually set you up for long-term success. When parts of your plan don't work out the way you thought, just adapt, but still with the end goal in mind. The person that is able to have the most adaptability will win, especially in this day and age.

Earlier I said that you should focus solely on the clouds and the dirt, the vision and the execution towards that vision, but there is one exception. In order to hold yourself accountable for your execution, and to continue fueling your flight towards the greater vision, you must have milestone goals. One thing that successful people say contributes greatly to their success is that they reflect. Each day they reflect what they accomplished and where they fell short. They celebrate even the small wins of that day so that they can remain motivated on their journey towards accomplishing their greater goals by seeing their progress. But at the same time, they are also very critical around where they may have fell short, and they figure out how they can be better for the next day. You need to reflect and track your progress with milestone goals, and like your overall end-goal, your milestone goals need to be super specific and quantifiable. Rather than saying that you want to get stronger, say that you want to be able to do fifty solid push-ups in a row by a certain date, and that to get there you will do fifty push-ups each morning, not necessarily in a row but over time, and then repeat that at night. Track your progress religiously, celebrate the small wins, but be critical around how you can improve, and you will crush it.

Your goals need to be super specific so that you know exactly what to do to get there. And you probably don't understand exactly how specific I mean, so let me share with you an example. Jim Carrey grew up poor. When his dad lost his job, his family got jobs as janitors and security guards at a factory while living in someone's backyard. Even Jim Carrey at the age of fifteen would come and work an eight-hour shift right after he got home from school, until he eventually dropped out of school a year later to try and pursue a career in comedy. At the age of nineteen he went to Hollywood with big dreams, but his goals weren't specific enough, and because of this, he fell short and didn't accomplish anything in particular. Alone, broke, and depressed without any idea what he should do, Jim Carrey made the decision that he would make it in Hollywood. He wrote a cheque for himself that was post-dated for approximately ten years later. The cheque was for 'acting services rendered', and he wrote the cheque for $10,000,000. Sure enough, approximately ten years later he got his big break when he debuted in 'Dumb and Dumber'. Like Jim Carrey did, you need to set your goals extremely high. Screw S.M.A.R.T. goals. You should set your goals so high that it seems impossible, and don't worry about how you will get there for now. Just set a date and a super specific goal, and then work towards actualizing that goal.

Frank W. Gunsaulus was a man who noticed a need for a fix of the current education system. He noticed a problem with the way that colleges were set up and how they functioned, and so he set out to fix that problem. It became his mission, his burning desire to one day become the head of his own college that he would start that would fill the gap in what current colleges were lacking. He said that the basis of his college would be around learning by doing. The only thing between him and his huge goal was money. Specifically, $1,000,000, which in his day was a huge sum of money. He had this desire at the top of his mind and he carried it with him wherever he went. He went to bed with the thought and woke up with it and carried it around with him wherever he went, at the top of his mind. This became his absolute obsession, but he had no idea where to accumulate the $1,000,000 that was needed to make his dream a reality. Unlike most people, he didn't give up on his dream even though he had no idea how to get his hands on the capital that he needed. Two years went by, and this obsession was still at the top of his mind. One Saturday, he decided that he had procrastinated long enough and that it was finally time for action. On that Saturday, he decided that no matter what, he was going to get his hands on $1,000,000 this week! He had absolutely no idea how this could be possible, but he knew that somehow, he would find a way. He had a definite purpose, and he laid out a super specific and quantifiable goal that had a timeline. He went to bed that night knowing that by the end of this coming week he would have the capital needed to start his own college. The next morning, he decided to hold a sermon, which he entitled 'What I Would do With a Million Dollars'. He stood up there and pitched his idea to an audience, sharing his great idea of how he could change the education system and start his own school based on learning from experience that would truly set his students up for success and fill the gap that was in the current education system. After pitching this idea, a man stood up and began walking up to the pulpit. He told him that he believed in his idea, and to prove his belief in the idea, he told Frank Gunsaulus that he could stop by his office the following morning where he would present him with $1,000,000.

Frank Gunsaulus said that when he finally made the decision and set a definite date that he would somehow get that million dollars that very week, something shifted inside of him. It felt like all of a sudden, he had access to the money that he required, and it felt like it had been waiting there all along, just waiting for him to be ready for it. All he needed to do was set that specific goal and tie it to a specific time. He had absolutely no idea how he would accomplish his goal, but somehow, he knew that by the end of that week, he would have in his possession the necessary $1,000,000. And sure enough, he did.

We must set our goals, and set them super high, but then make those goals as specific as possible. Whatever that goal may be, set a specific date for it, and the exact thing that you want to accomplish, and you will feel this shift that all along your biggest goals were waiting for you to unlock them, and all you had to do was get specific around what exactly you wanted, and when.

There is a strong, direct relationship between the difficulty of goals and the likelihood we will achieve them. And on top of that, you will also have greater motivation, creativity and satisfaction when going after these huge goals. Lay out your biggest goal that may seem impossible, and then 10x that goal, because I assure you that you can do whatever you set your mind to as long as you don't get caught up in the clouds, being the grand vision, and you actual spend most of your time in the dirt, putting in the work that will start that domino effect towards your biggest goals.

6 FORGET ABOUT YOUR WEAKNESSES. FOCUS ON YOUR STRENGTHS.

I am sure that people have told you that everyone has weaknesses, and you probably have your own weaknesses that you are probably very aware of. The average belief is to try to fix your weaknesses, or to at least improve in the areas in your life where you fall short. And so people take this and run with it, and they end up spending their whole lives just trying to fix their weaknesses that they see as gaps in their potential. They see their weaknesses as the missing pieces to what will make them a successful person. It seems like common sense to spend the majority of your time trying to fix your flaws so that you can be better as a whole, without those weaknesses dragging you down. But I assure you that when people spend their lives focused solely on focusing on fixing their weaknesses, in the end all they accomplish is becoming a well-rounded and all around average human being.

I don't know about you, but in my case, I want to become more than just average. I will never settle for only being average, and I think that that is what will allow me to always strive to learn and grow and become better than I was yesterday. This is the mindset that you need to succeed. You should never settle for who you are today. Sure, you should be happy with who you are, but what I mean by this is that you should always strive to be better. You could choose to accept where things are, or you could set the bar high and work towards accomplishing greatness. Instead of settling for who you are and just working on trying to improve your weaknesses, you should forget about your weaknesses and instead go all in on your strengths.

Confucius once said that "the man who chases two rabbits catches none". You need to understand that you can either have greatness in one area or widespread mediocrity. The general outlook of society is for us to focus on improving our weaknesses, but in doing so all that you are doing is working towards widespread mediocrity. Instead of sucking at one thing and having a lot of potential in another area, you forget about the one thing that you are really good at and spend all of your time on improving the thing that you suck at, and in doing so you bring your skill-level up on the area that you naturally aren't good at so that you reach the point where you become average, and in doing so you neglect the area that you could have potential in, and so that plateau's as well, leaving you with being a socially accepted, well-rounded person who will forever remain average. Would you rather have widespread mediocrity, or would you like to unlock your limitless potential in the area that you excel at?

Take the example of school. Let's imagine that you are in grade 10, and you love English class and with this passion you've found yourself at the top of your class. Science on the other hand is your least favorite subject. You struggle to understand the concepts that you are learning in Science, and the small percentage that you do understand isn't super crystallized because you just don't find it interesting whatsoever. This disinterest and natural lack of skill has led to you barely passing grade 10 science. Your parents have been making you spend the majority of your time focusing on improving your grade in science, and so in doing so you have been neglecting English because you simply don't have enough extra time left over to continue developing your skills of writing. By the end of the year, when your report card comes in, you will probably find that you did end up getting your science grade up, but in turn the grade in your English class has been getting worse. You end up crippling your success and limiting yourself from accomplishing greatness in the area of the language arts, and ultimately you end up achieving nothing but widespread mediocrity.

In the above example, the way to unlock your limitless potential is to focus on what you are actually good at and what you really have a chance in achieving success in. Let's be real, if your grade in science is that bad and you just have absolutely no interest in the subject at all, then you aren't going to pursue a career in the sciences. In writing on the other hand, you could have a great shot to achieve greatness with your own book or blog or in being a journalist or something around the field of language arts. Instead of trying to focus on improving your weaknesses that won't play a part in your future whatsoever and allowing your strengths to suffer in doing so, you could go all in on your strength of writing so that you can stand out from the crowd in that area and that will ultimately drive your success. And of course, in this example, it is still important to get all of your grades up so that you can keep your overall GPA up, but you get the point from this analogy.

Remember that you need to make a judgment call that can mean the difference between standing out and blending in with the other wanna-be's and that is whether you want to achieve greatness in what it is that you are good at, or widespread mediocrity. The choice is up to you, and I think that although the latter option may seem like the more common sensical thing to do, in order to truly unlock your limitless potential, you need to triple down on your strengths and forget about your weaknesses. Unless the areas that you are weak at play an important role in accomplishing your greater vision, then you should forget about them altogether, but if you absolutely need them to compliment your core strengths, then that is the only exception.

You need to understand that when you focus on investing in your strengths rather than fixing your deficiencies, then you will multiply your potential for growth and eventual overall success. Not only will focusing on your strengths allow you to achieve massive success in that one thing that you are focusing on, but it will also allow you to feel more fulfilled and achieve much greater work. Earlier I talked about the two parts that allow you to get into flow states and those are a combination of both challenge and skill. To refresh, if you are not skilled enough to do something then you will feel overwhelmed and incapable. If you are skilled enough but you aren't experiencing enough challenge to match that level of skill, then you will feel lost and like you aren't serving a greater purpose, and ultimately you will feel a lack of overall fulfillment, like what we were talking about in the chapter on getting outside of your comfort zone in order to feel fulfilled. So, in relation to your strengths, you not only need to go after your strengths so that you can escalate your success potential in that area, but also so that you will also get into flow states more consistently due to the skill level that you have in that area, and the challenges that you are able to face head on won't stop you or cause you to become burnt out because of the passion that you have for what it is that you are doing. If you don't agree with what I am talking about, let's take a look at the statistics because those don't lie: people who have the opportunity to focus on their strengths in their careers are six times more likely to feel engaged in what they are doing, thus escalating their performance even further and getting you into that upward spiral that we talked about in the first chapter.

At a young age, everyone is told that they can be whoever they want to be. Although I agree that you can do whatever you set your mind to, you need to be extremely self-aware when you are going after your strengths. You need to go all in on the things that are actually your strengths, not the things that you wish were. For me personally, even if I really wanted to be a professional basketball player and I practiced for hours every day, I still wouldn't have a very good chance, simply because I don't have that strength. You need to be self-aware about what you are naturally good at and then go after that thing. This may take a little while to find out what your true strengths are, or you could know right away. But either way, it is important to try a lot of things while you can, especially while you are young, until you figure out the thing that you are best at.

The problem with this is that a lot of people will come to a cross-road when they read this advice, where they have tried a lot of things and they've narrowed it down to a couple of things that they are super good at. They know that either of these paths could potentially lead to them unlocking their limitless potential, and they know that they can't go down both paths. My advice to you would be to not overthink it. Just make the decision and run with it. Decisiveness is a key factor towards your success, and without it you will lose.

I know it can be hard when you are faced with a decision, and you will never know if you go ahead in one direction what the other path could have led to. Most people stop at these cross-roads. They become paralyzed by their indecisiveness and this leads to them not moving forward in any one direction. If you are ever faced with a cross-road like this, don't overthink it. Just choose one option and go all in, and don't worry about looking back and dwelling. Just keep moving forward and growing your strengths.

The way to succeed is to forget about the areas that you fall short in and instead focus on developing who you already are. Gary Vaynerchuk said it himself: "Focus on your strengths, not your weaknesses". And he didn't just say it, he is a living example of how focusing on his strengths and forgetting about his weaknesses lead to him unlocking his limitless potential, which is still exponentially growing by the way.

In school, Gary Vaynerchuk was your classic D and F student who paid little attention in school. His mind was instead always on how he could make money and build his strategy, from ripping flowers out of people's gardens and selling them back to them, to flipping baseball cards and bringing in tens of thousands of dollars as a teenager, to eventually growing his family's wine business by going all in on his natural strength of understanding consumer behaviour and predicting the market, which by the way, he says is thanks to him not actually predicting what people will do, but seeing what is already happening and acting on it. It's that simple. He allowed his strengths to see that video was an emerging way that people were going to consume content, and he acted on this by deploying his strengths to start a show called Wine Library TV which multiplied the revenue of this brick and mortar business through social interaction.

Gary Vaynerchuk is extremely self-aware. He knew that he didn't fit into the mold that society provides us with and he knew that he was different. Instead of doing what most people would have done in his situation and focused on working hard at school to improve his weaknesses which would allow him to achieve widespread mediocrity, he went all in on what he knew he could achieve success in. He knew that he wouldn't be the type of person that would learn from reading and consuming, but rather he learned from executing. He took action, hustled, and learned from the experience and the inevitable failures along the way. In fact, he truly doesn't believe in traditional learning which shows by the fact that he is close to reaching the point where he will have written and published more bestselling books than he has read, and this is all because he had the self-awareness necessary to assess what his strengths were and take action on them, leaving his weaknesses in the dust and never looking back. And look where it got him.

Take the time now to become extremely self-aware and figure out what your strengths are, and then take action on those strengths and focus on improving who you actually are rather than trying to become someone that you aren't by working on your weaknesses. Don't sacrifice your limitless potential by spending your time on trying to fix the areas that you fall short on. If you spend your time on trying to fix your weaknesses, your strengths will plateau. You will achieve widespread mediocrity. Or, you can take action today to achieve greatness in that one thing that you know you are naturally great at, and never look back.

7 MOTIVATION IS TEMPORARY. MOTIVE IS LASTING.

I bet this scenario feels all too familiar to you. You watch a movie or listen to a song or a speech or you just wake up on the absolute right side of the bed, and suddenly you feel super motivated, like nothing could possibly stop you. You feel absolutely invincible and ready to crush all of your goals by tackling any obstacles that could cross your path head on. You feel absolutely relentless and unstoppable, like in that moment you have already unlocked your limitless potential. You decide in that moment that today is the day that you are going to finally stop saying one day, and that today will in fact be your day one. You decide that you are going to go all in on working towards your dreams, and you are done procrastinating and you are ready to just go all in.

Sure enough, after a couple of days of absolute focus, at most, you eventually find yourself back in the very rut that you started from. And then after a few weeks of just going through the motions, you suddenly get that motivation back, whether it be from some quote that you saw while scrolling through Instagram or a song that you heard on the radio that really pumped you up and inspired you. But after a couple of hours of feeling absolutely motivated, you find yourself right back where you started once more, just living reactively and drifting through life. You know that you want to achieve success and unlock your limitless potential, but it seems impossible to ever achieve the stamina needed to put in the work to achieve that success. There is no way that you will make it if you rely solely on the classic form of motivation that comes to you at random times and fires you up, but then fades shortly after. Luckily though, you can proactively create motivation, and not only the kind of motivation that you constantly need to feed and fuel, but rather a more lasting kind of motivation. Although motivation is temporary, motive is lasting.

If you rely on spurts of motivation, you won't gain lasting momentum. But if you take the time to articulate a clear motive for what you are doing, and you allow that to guide you, then you will be able to create lasting motivation that will drive you. Instead of having to push yourself to put in the work, the motive that you set for yourself will pull you towards it. It will be the source of your energy that allows you to jump out of bed each morning, ready to tackle the challenges that could lay ahead but that will ultimately lead to the accomplishment of that grand vision or motive. This is similar to what I talked about in the chapter on goals. You need to set huge goals so that they can pull you by their monumental gravitational field. This is similar to your motive, which needs to be a huge vision that drives you up in the clouds, that allows you to feel motivated enough to put in the work necessary down in the dirt of it all.

Not only should you have a clear motive for your own life and who you are as a person and who you are striving to become, but the same should apply for any organizations that you are a part of. Whether you are starting your own company, or you work for a specific organization, you need a clearly defined motive. And even if this doesn't apply directly to you, it is still important.

Whenever a company is founded, it is almost always because the founder had a light bulb moment when they finally decided to put their fists down and solve the problem that was right in front of them, whatever that may be. This moment is extremely important, and it should be frequently articulated to the employees because this is what should be the motive of the company, the driving force that guides action and that provides a framework and a state of mind to base day to day decisions off of. The problem is that this moment is often lost in time, as the founder eventually moves on and the company grows, and eventually it gets to the point where the company lies and operates solely in the dirt, being the execution of strategy to overcome competition, and they focus solely on numbers and breaking even and getting a profit. It loses sight of the actual vision that started the company, being the clouds. The company needs to operate day to day in the dirt, but in order to achieve long-term success, it must still consistently be reminded of the clouds that can guide these day to day decisions.

A great example of a company that has been able to allow a clear motive to drive its all-time success is none other than Apple. When Steve Jobs first started Apple, he had a vision of giving the power to the people to have the freedom to think differently and ultimately change the world. Simon Sinek talks about this idea in his book, Start With Why. The reason that Apple has had so much success and has reigned over Android for all these years isn't because it has the best software necessarily. In fact, Apple's own employees will for the most part not disagree that Android produces better software with more functionality. But Apple isn't about that. They sell high quality electronics, but that isn't actually what they are selling. Apple is selling the ability to go against the status quote and think differently, and ultimately change the world, because as Steve Jobs said it himself, "the people who are crazy enough to think that they can change the world are the ones who do". Apple isn't only selling what they physically have. In their marketing campaigns, Apple doesn't talk about the detailed specifications of their product.

As Simon Sinek said in his TEDx Talk, "Here is how Apple actually communicates: 'Everything we do, we believe in challenging the status quo. We believe in thinking differently. The way that we challenge the status quo is by making our products beautifully designed, simple to use, and user friendly. We just happen to make great computers. Want to buy one?' On the other hand, if Apple was like everyone else, a marketing message might sound something like this: 'We make great computers. They are beautifully designed, easy to use, and user friendly. Want to buy one?'". As you can see, the reason why Simon Sinek's book is entitled 'Start With Why' is because that is exactly what he suggests we do. The reason that Apple is successful is because, like in the first example, they lead with the greater why or motive behind what they do, which inspires action, and then they lead into the how, and then end with exactly what it is that they are selling. Android does the second example, where they lead in with what they are selling instead of starting with the greater why, and this is bland and doesn't inspire action. If you start with why, and you allow that greater motive to pull you towards unlocking your limitless potential, then nothing will be able to stop you, and you will also be able to inspire others.

This idea of starting with why applies not only to companies and organizations but to us as well. We should have a clearly defined greater motive that we can allow to guide our day to day decisions. We should always have a definite major purpose that is the paradigm of our life, and this should provide us with the fuel in the form of lasting motivation that is necessary to achieve our dreams. Starting with why and having a clear motive or definite major purpose is the main factor of success, as a person as well as in an organization. If you have a cloudy end goal, then you will find yourself aimlessly drifting through life and not gaining any traction and not gaining any meaningful distance in any specific direction. If you have a clear and definite major purpose, then you will be able to achieve your goals so much faster because you can have a streamlined focus that takes you straight to that location. That is why Apple has had so much global success, and it is also how people that you look up to as idols have gotten to their success.

A great example of someone who had a definite major purpose that drove them straight to unlocking their limitless potential and accomplishing their goals is the story of Edwin C. Barnes. The story of Edwin C. Barnes is a powerful story of how a clear motive can lead to you accomplishing anything and overcoming any setbacks that may come along your journey. Edwin C. Barnes went from rags to riches, all because of a clear purpose that he let drive him.

It all started with an idea. Edwin C. Barnes had come from a poor upbringing and he was living broke and in a seemingly hopeless situation. The only thing that he had going for him was the clear major purpose of working with Thomas Edison, the famous inventor. He didn't want to work for Thomas Edison, but rather he wanted to work alongside him. And even though he had nothing that would point in the direction of this motive actually becoming his reality, he somehow knew that he would be able to make it happen, and this motive gave him hope for the future.

Edwin C. Barnes didn't even have enough money to pay for the train ticket to travel to Edison's lab, but he was determined and he would not let that stop him. He decided to just go for it and so he hopped onto a freight train and hoped for the best. He had a clear motive and he allowed that to give him the motivation necessary to keep going even when the times got tough.

Edwin C. Barnes finally made it to Thomas Edison's lab and presented himself to the great inventor himself. Although he wasn't able to immediately achieve his definite major purpose of working with Thomas Edison, he was able to start working in the lab and he eventually worked his way up to the position that he was looking for through his persistence, hard work, and creative ideas. Looking back, Thomas Edison said that "He stood there before me, looking like an ordinary tramp, *but there was something in the expression of his face which conveyed the impression that he was determined to get what he had come after.* I had learned, from years of experience with men, that when a man really DESIRES a thing so deeply that he is willing to stake his entire future on a single turn of the wheel in order to get it, he is sure to win. I gave him the opportunity he asked for, *because I saw he had made up his mind to stand by until he succeeded.* Subsequent events proved that no mistake was made."

The reason that Edwin C. Barnes allowed his motive to become a reality is because he allowed that to be his burning and unquenchable desire. He was relentless and would not stop until he had accomplished his motive and made his definite major purpose his reality. You cannot only have a clear motive and expect to achieve success, but instead you need to actually allow that motive to become a burning desire, and then actually take action on that burning desire and have the relentlessness to not stop until you have created that given reality for yourself, just like Edwin C. Barnes did.

You need to have a clear motive and it needs to be an actual sincere motive. If your motive is to achieve fame and fortune then you will never get there. First of all, that isn't clear enough. You should have a clearly defined amount of money that you would like to acquire and the date that you want to have it by, just like Jim Carrey did in the story that we talked about earlier. But for the most part, this shouldn't be your motive. If your motive is of a sincere intent then the money will likely come as a by-product if you allow the sincere desires to motivate you.

I bet that most of you reading this book actually haven't heard of Samuel Pierpont Langley, but I am sure that you have heard of the Wright Brothers. In fact, not only have you likely heard of the Wright brothers but you have probably also heard of their story, or at least part of it revolving around the fact that they were able to create and fly the very first airplane. What you probably know is only actually part of the story though.

Samuel Pierpont Langley was on track to engineer and pilot the first plane. He had the exact ingredients that anyone would be consider to be factors to achieving success. He had so much wealth to fund his work towards creating the first plane, and he also had the support of many important people as well as an audience eagerly watching to see what would happen.

Samuel Pierpont Langley had the wealth and the fame necessary to achieve success, but the thing that he was lacking was a sincere and burning desire. All that he was after was increasing his wealth and fame. He just wanted even more fame and fortune, and so his desires were not sincere. Although he wanted to accomplish this monumental task of engineering flight, his mind wasn't right and he didn't have the right motives to truly motivate and propel him towards his success. Psychologists have correctly said that "when one is truly ready for a thing, it puts in its appearance." The problem with Samuel Pierpont Langley is that he was not truly ready to accomplish the task at hand.

Meanwhile in the background, as all eyes were on Pierpont Langley, there were two brothers who had no fame, in fact no one at all was watching. And they had little to no money to fund their ventures. Although Pierpont Langley had the things that would seem to be the necessary ingredients to achieve success, and the Wright Brothers had none of these necessary ingredients, the Wright Brothers were still the ones that succeeded in the end. These ingredients that seem essential for success didn't actually play any part in the outcomes of these people, and they never really have if you look close enough. These ingredients for success are just surface level answers, but to find the true drivers of success you need to look deeper, and these driving forces that lead to success lie in the universal principles of this book, and specifically for this example it lies in the principle that although motivation is temporary, motive is lasting. If you have a clear motive and you allow that sincere motive to guide your day to day decisions, then nothing will be able to stop you.

The reason that the Wright Brothers were able to succeed and accomplish their motive is because they let their genuine curiosity lead to their discovery. They had a sincere motive, and rather than being after fame and fortune, they genuinely wanted to help move the human race forward and change the world for the better. And because this was their driving purpose, they were able to accomplish what they set out to do, and no limit of resources or surface level obstacles could stop their motive that fueled their determination and persistence.

In whatever way you apply what you have learned from this chapter, the main thing that you need to take away is that you need to have a definite major purpose so that you can allow that to drive you and provide you with everlasting motivation. You need your definite major purpose to drive you straight towards the outcome that you are after, and you need that definite major purpose to turn into a burning desire that will allow you to become invincible in your pursuit of this definite major purpose.

8 NEVER, NEVER, NEVER GIVE UP

Winston Churchill once said to "never, never, never give up" and this simple quote is almost more important than anything and can and will mean the difference between you breaking through and unlocking your limitless potential, and you remaining average.

In the story in the previous chapter, I talked about how Edwin C. Barnes was persistent and driven, and he would not accept failure. He was determined to achieve what he had set out to do, and Thomas Edison saw this fire within him and this played a huge part in why Thomas Edison gave him a chance. The ability to be persistent and never give up is more important than anything, especially in this day and age where persistence, drive, and focus are more important factors of success, and can and often do surpass natural talent or skill. So often you see people who surpass others even when the odds were against them, and this is because the only thing they had going for them was persistence and determination and the ability to keep going even when times get tough.

Someone with little talent but the ability to keep going and never give up will overcome someone else with limitless talent but that lacks the persistence to keep hustling. Always. There are no exceptions. Persistence, although it doesn't necessarily seem cool, is extremely important. Oftentimes it just so happens that right when you are about to finally achieve a breakthrough, you feel a lot of pressure holding you back. Most people quit when success is right around the corner because that is when times usually get the toughest, and you will never know how close you were. If you feel like giving up, keep going because you can never know how close you were to achieving the success that you were after, and rather than quitting and then looking back and dwelling on what could have happened, you can trudge forward and find out for yourself. The worst kind of regret will always be around the things that you didn't do. This creates lasting regret that will never leave you alone. If, on the other hand, you did decide to keep going and you found that it was a complete waste of time, then you will still feel regret but it won't be lasting regret. And like I said, you can never know. It is just as likely that you will achieve success and it will all be worth it in the end.

As I said, the pressure gets the strongest when success is right around the corner, and this idea is certainly true in the case of R. U. Darby. Napoleon Hill once said that "One of the most common causes of failure is the habit of quitting when one is overtaken by *temporary defeat*. Every person is guilty of this mistake at one time or another." In R. U Darby's case, you will find that sometimes you will quit when you are literally three feet from gold.

R. U. Darby had the desire to go dig for gold in the gold rush days in hopes of coming home with riches. Little did he know that what he would walk away from that experience wouldn't be gold, but rather a lesson much more valuable than any amount of gold. R. U. Darby dug for gold for weeks of hard work, all to no avail. Luckily though, he had a clear motive and lust for gold that was able to drive him to keep going and not give up. Finally, he was rewarded when he found what he was looking for. In finding the gold ore, he decided to cover up where he had found it and he headed back home so that he could acquire the money needed from friends and family to be able to pay for the proper equipment necessary to mine the gold.

When they came back with the equipment that they would be able to use to bring their new-found riches to the surface, they began to drill. But as they dug deeper to where they originally saw the gold ores, they found that it was no longer there. After a little while of frantic searching, R. U. Darby decided that he was truly the unluckiest man ever. He believed that his gold had simply disappeared right from his grasp, and so he accepted defeat and headed home feeling extremely disappointed.

Before heading home, they decided to sell the machinery that they had acquired. They were able to sell it for a couple hundred dollars to a junk man, but little did they know that what they were really giving away was millions of dollars in gold. This junk man was smart enough to seek out expert advice and so he called a mining engineer to come and take a look at the mine. Upon further calculation, they discovered that the fault lines had caused the vein of gold to move only slightly. In fact, the vein of gold was literally only three feet away from the place where R. U. Darby had given up. He was three feet away from gold, literally three feet from acquiring millions of dollars, and he gave up.

You may remember that earlier I had said that R. U. Darby would walk away from that gold rush without any gold, but rather with a lesson that was worth more than any amount of gold. From his experience of giving up when he was only three feet from gold, R. U. Darby was able to learn the importance of persistence the hard way. He also eventually learned that the power of the mind and the principles that you learn and follow are much more important than any amount of gold, and they could potentially provide you with much more riches than any amount of gold ever could. Gold can be taken away or lost, but you will always keep with you the lessons that you have learned from your experiences, and the knowledge that you've accumulated along the way.

Napoleon Hill said "Mr. Darby recouped his loss many times over, *when he made the discovery* that DESIRE can be transmuted into gold". The power of persistence is much more important than gold, and it is something that R. U. Darby was able to acquire from his experiences. From that moment forward, he would have the drive and determination necessary to accomplish anything that he wanted in life, because he decided that he would never stop three feet from gold again. This became his new mantra: "I stopped three feet from gold, but I will never stop *because men say 'no'* when I ask them to buy insurance."

Yes, he decided he would take what he learned and apply it to selling insurance, and although it doesn't sound super interesting, he was still able to excel at what he did by applying this simple principle, and you can too. Not only will the ability to persist help you in working toward and achieving your dreams and goals, but it will also help you to be able to be a better salesperson and really just a better all-around person in whatever it is that you do.

With this lesson that R. U. Darby learned, he was able to apply it and use it to sell millions of insurances year after year. This lesson that he was able to learn provided him with the right mindset and drive to achieve lasting success rather than a one-time lottery that he would have likely lost with time, because as we will talk about in the next chapter, it isn't about the million dollars that you earn, but what you have to become to do so. That is why so many lottery winners end up going broke – because they can't handle the wealth because they haven't earned it.

When Napoleon Hill was talking about success coming right after temporary failure that often makes people quit, he said that "their greatest success came just one step beyond the point at which defeat had overtaken them. Failure is a trickster with a keen sense of irony and cunning. It takes great delight in tripping one when success is almost within reach."

Don't let failure trick you. Be happy when you find yourself confronted with some opposition in the form of obstacles along the way. Take failure as a sign that success is just around the corner.

The way to achieve success and to truly be persistent in everything that you do means that you need to be more than just passionate. Being passionate is sort of like having temporary motivation, rather than having the lasting motive like we talked about earlier. Most people rely on passion and their own willpower and they hope that they wind up somewhere meaningful, but that is very rarely the case. You need to be passionate about what it is that you are doing, but you can't rely only on passion. The problem with passion is that one day you might feel passionate about one thing and then the next day it's completely different, and so you don't gain any meaningful traction in any direction.

The way to achieve success is to combine your passion with determination. You need to be passionate, but this passion needs to be proactively directed in a specific direction so that you can gain some distance in that direction. You need to not only be passionate, but you also need to infuse that passion with determination so that you will be able to keep going and stay focused in that one area, rather than constantly shifting the things that you are passionate about. When you are determined you need to focus on that one thing that you are determined to accomplish, and then you allow your passion to fuel you in the short-term.

Passion is able to fuel you in the short-term, but if you only rely on passion then you will constantly be shifting the direction that you are travelling, and so on top of your short-term passion, you also need determination that will drive you in the long-term. When you have determination, it provides you with a clear path of where you are going so that you can go straight to that destination and allow your passion to fuel you along the way.

You should have a clear destination and be determined to get there, and that end goal should never change. But, don't worry if you experience temporary defeat along the way. The goal should never change, but the plan to get there should be extremely flexible and malleable. If you don't have a clear end-goal in the form of determination, then you will wander aimlessly through life, relying on spurts of passion that get you nowhere. And then on the other hand, if you don't allow any flexibility on the path of getting to the end goal, then you will accept temporary defeat and make it permanent by quitting.

There will always be a tipping point in persistence. When you work hard at something, you start off excited but eventually a gradual decline inevitably begins as you start to lose interest and it seems hopeless, and you feel burnt out and ready to quit. Usually this happens right when you are just a few feet from gold, and the only way to succeed in life is to stick to it and be persistent. Although passion is a powerful driving force, it can easily be fickle and shift from thing to thing, and so one day you are feeling passionate about starting a certain business but then a little while later you lose interest and start something different. If you try to rely solely on passion, you will never get anywhere. Instead, you need to rely on something a little different called *determination.* You see, the difference between passion and determination is a fine line, but it can be the differentiator between success and failure. Passion can vary from thing to thing and it can change as you grow and develop overtime, and it can also change daily depending on how you are feeling that day. If you rely on passion then you will easily drift from one thing to the next and never gain traction. You need to understand that the quote by Confucius where he said "The man who chases two rabbits catches none", applies here as well. In order to achieve success, you need to focus on one thing, and be determined to accomplish that one thing and allow that to be your laser vision.

9 WITH A LEVER LONG ENOUGH YOU CAN MOVE THE WORLD

Earlier on in the book I mentioned the business that I started when I was nine-years-old that I was able to go on the national television show Dragons Den with. The whole idea of this business revolves around my card game, Doogoods, as well as the assembly programs that I do for elementary schools to spread the Doogoods movement. The whole idea of the cards and the movement is to raise the next generation as Upstanders instead of bystanders by making doing good fun and kindness cool. Instead of being anti-bullying, we focus on being pro-kindness, which in turn will end bullying as a by-product. The reason that I am telling you about this is because with this card game, I'm not necessarily focusing on trying to get everyone to come together to spend a year trying to do some big thing like building a school in Africa. Although that would certainly make a huge impact, I believe that that is really only a surface level fix. All it is doing is putting a band-aid on the larger problem, when the way to fix this is to focus on raising the next generation the right way, by raising them in the right atmosphere where they are encouraged to and have fun completing even the simplest of acts of kindness.

The thing is, when these kids are completing these simple acts of kindness, a chemical called oxytocin is released in the person doing the simple act of kindness, the person on the receiving end, and even everyone around watching. Oxytocin is a chemical that, when released, makes you feel happier, healthier, and ultimately *wanting to do more good.* So, when you complete a simple act of kindness, it makes you feel good by releasing this positive high, and so when kids grow up having fun completing these simple acts of kindness, they grow up literally getting addicted to being kind. They love the feeling it brings them, and so they seek after opportunities when they grow up in that reality. And then each time that they complete a simple act of kindness, it makes everyone around them feel good as well, and it makes those people want to do more good as well. And some of them might not, but there will be people who will take that feeling and actually take action on it, spreading this chain reaction of kindness even further, and so you can only imagine how this can literally multiply over time and it will do so exponentially until eventually we will have an epidemic of kindness, and so starting with that one small act of kindness, even just a smile, we can ultimately change the world for the better.

The reason that I tell you this story is to demonstrate the power that simple things can have to create huge outcomes. The way to change the world is to sometimes stop thinking so big and think small so that everyone can easily complete a simple act of kindness, and then this starts a chain reaction that starts the snowball effect that leads to eventually knocking over huge things. Although thinking big is extremely important in the clouds, in the greater vision, you then need to start small in the dirt, being the execution of it all. When you start small and find ways to engineer a chain reaction, you can engineer success and knock over huge things by looking in the right places and finding the small actions with huge outcomes. The reason that I tell you this story is because it is a great example of when Archimedes said "Give me a lever long enough and a place to stand and I will move the world". You can change the world if you are able to leverage the right things to create massive effects from small things, which is extremely scalable, and this applies to us and our time and productivity which will lead to our ultimate and inevitable success if we are able to leverage this principle. The one variable to success is having enough time, and time is a really important variable that I kind of want to talk about this concept of time.

Every single person on Earth has the same twenty-four hours each day. Bill Gates and Steve Jobs and Mark Zuckerberg all have the same twenty-four hours every day as you and I do. You simply can't get around it. Time will always pass and you can't get time back. The only thing that you can control is how you spend your time. I am sure at some point in time you have said that you don't have the time to do something, but that is just an excuse to accept mediocrity. You say that you don't have enough time to go after your dreams, but it isn't actually a matter of lack of time but rather a lack of priorities. I bet you didn't know that the average person spends more time on laptops and phones than they do sleeping, which is almost nine hours on devices each day. That ends up being more than two-thousand hours spent on devices in a year. And I understand that a lot of this time could be doing actual meaningful work, but the average season of TV takes probably around ten hours to watch, so I want you to think of all of those TV shows that you have watched in the past year. Imagine how much time that would add up to be? Imagine if you used this time to instead work on meaningful things such as working towards your goals. You need to set your priorities straight – would you rather waste your life away behind the screen, or would you rather use that time and end up being the person that people see on TV. You can't do both. Time is all about priorities, because we all get the same twenty-four hours but the differentiator is what you do with that time. Don't fall into reactivity to your surroundings. You need to engineer your time to get the most of it, because although time does fly, you are the pilot.

Now that you understand my stance on time, that although you can't control time you can control what you do with it, and now that you hopefully have shattered the limiting belief that you don't have the time, we can move onto the way to maximize the outputs of what you are doing. Since you have a finite amount of time, you need to figure out how to get the most out of what you are doing. Put simply, the way to be productive is by auditing your inputs and getting rid of the things that you are wasting your time on that aren't producing results that match the time put in, and then find and focus on the things that you are able to do that provide you with huge outputs that overshadow the work put in.

I am sure that you have heard of the Pareto principle, more commonly known as the 80/20 principle, which states that in most events, 80% of the effects come from 20% of the causes. This idea was first noted when Vilfredo Pareto, an Italian economist, who noticed that in Italy, approximately 80% of the land was owned by 20% of the population. Later on, Joseph M. Juran, a management consultant, noticed that this principle can be applied to almost anything in relation to cause and effect, and so he was the one that coined the principle and named it after

Vilfredo Pareto who first noticed this idea.

This principle can be found all around you. 80% of the wealth of the world belongs to 20% of the people (except probably more like 99% belongs to 1%). 80% of value is produced from 20% of the effort. 80% of sales come from 20% of customers. 80% of income comes from 20% of products. And each of these examples also has a flip side, for example: Although 80% of value is produced from 20% of the effort, there is also 20% of the value that comes from 80% of the effort. And in Vilfredo Pareto's example, although 80% of property is owned by 20% of people, there is also therefore the other 20% of the property owned by 80% of the people.

Wow. That is a lot to take in, but the main thing that you need to take away from this idea of the 80/20 principle is that 80% of the effect comes from 20% of causes. There will always be the small amount of effort, the 20%, that will produce the biggest outcomes, the 80%. And then there will also be the less effective things where you spend 80% of your time and that time only produces 20% of your overall results. So, what you need to take away from this is that you need to cut out the causes that take up a lot of your time but produce a much lesser effect, and you need to focus on the causes that don't take much time but that produce a much bigger effect or result. If you do the math then you will see that if you cut out the time wasters, and you focused 100% on the causes that produced 80% of your results when you only focused on those 20% of the time, then you would find that when focusing 100%, those would then produce 400% more results, thus multiplying your overall results by four when you cut out the less effective causes and focus solely on the ones that produce the greatest effects. This brings me back to Archimedes saying that with a lever long enough, he could move the world. By only working hard, you could never do so, but if you take a strategic approach then it is theoretically possible.

The way to achieve maximum productivity is all about not only working harder, but working smarter as well, and coming at it with the right angle and the proper uses of your time that produce the biggest results. The way to be productive really comes down to one key thing, and that is elimination. Like I said in the example of the 80/20 principle, the way to maximize your time is to cut out the ineffective inputs and have tunnel visions on the inputs that provide you with substantial outputs

The way to be productive and get a lot more done and truly move the needle towards what you want to get done relies mainly on eliminating things. Elimination is a key element of productivity – instead of thinking that you need to overwhelm yourself with tactics and strategies and consuming tons of content on your internet that will somehow have the secret to master productivity, all you really need to do is eliminate. And when I say that you need to eliminate, I don't only mean eliminating the inputs that don't produce significant outputs. You not only need to focus on the inputs that actually matter, but then you also need to understand that by working less you can get more done.

I know this sounds super counterintuitive. By working less, how are you going to get more done? As a society we believe that in order to get a lot done we need to work longer hours, but this is actually not true at all. In order to be truly productive when you actually are working, you need to take the time to rest and get your energy up so that you can be more productive instead of dragging on at a slow pace. And when I say rest, I don't mean that you should do mind rotting activities like saying that you are resting while you sit and watch TV or things like that. When you are resting, what you should really be doing is meaningful things that allow your mind to wander and get creative without you even knowing it. Earlier we talked about how your subconscious mind loosely wanders while you sleep and connects the dots so that it sets you up for prime creativity right when you wake up in the morning. You can also allow your subconscious mind to connect the dots between the things that are on your mind, and your surroundings to come up with new and innovative ideas, but it will only do so if you don't have anything on your working memory.

In case you forgot, your working memory means your short-term memory, and it is usually filled with what you are doing right in that moment, whether it be writing an email or thinking about the things that you have to do. And when your working memory is focused on these short-term things, it doesn't have any room left for your subconscious mind to wander loosely and come up with creative breakthroughs. If you take the time to disconnect from your work and go walk outside for example, even just for a couple of minutes, it allows your subconscious mind to loosely wander and come up with creative ideas relating to what you were just working on. That is why if you feel stuck, it is a great idea to get up and take a break and reflect.

Elimination is the key to productivity, and so instead of forcing yourself to work non-stop long hours, you should allow yourself to take breaks that allow your subconscious mind to come up with creative conclusions relating to what you were just working on, and this also allows your mind to regenerate and rest and be ready to go full force once you get back into it.

When working out, shorter but more intensive bursts of exercise are much more effective, and then after that you should take a break to allow your muscles to rest and recover, and in this recovery is when they actually grow. If you were to always be just kind of working out on and off and never get into super high intensity, but then also never provide your muscles adequate time to rest and recover, then you will end up wasting a lot more time while producing lesser results. This is how most people go about their workdays. They go to work and they work for eight hours of somewhat focused but not fully engaged work, and especially near the end of the day it gets to the point where they are just being dragged through the work without being engaged whatsoever. There are countries, however, such as Luxembourg, where they only work around thirty hours a week unlike the standard over forty hours that us Canadians work, and they end up actually being more productive and getting more done and making more money in the time that they are working.

The people in countries where they work less are able to be absolutely focused and engaged when they are working, and they don't get to the point where they burn out and then they have time to rest and recover and get back at it the next day with the same fire. They have high intense working periods and then adequate time to recover and get creative insight for the next day. Oftentimes the way to get more done can be by doing less, but when you are doing that work you are high intensely working and absolutely focused and deeply engaged, and then once they stop working they are able to disconnect and rest and recover, which is when their subconscious loosely wanders, leading them to creative connections and ideas.

When you are focused, you should also not necessarily work all the way straight through. It is important to take short breaks in between work to reflect and connect ideas from more of a bird's eye view by getting away from the smaller details of what you are doing. A great way to do this is to use the Pomodoro Technique.

Francesco Cirillo was a university student in the late 1980's, and when he was doing his work he would use a kitchen timer that just so happened to be shaped as a tomato. He would chop up his work into high intensity intervals of time with this kitchen timer. He would set it for twenty-five minutes of absolute focused work with zero distractions, and then he would allow himself a five-minute break. Then after the five-minute break he would get back into working hard.

When he would be in his twenty-five minutes high intensity working periods, he would allow himself no lee-way for distractions whatsoever. In this time, he wouldn't check his phone or email or anything at all. He would be absolutely 100% engaged in what he was doing. And then once he finished this focus block of time, he would allow his mind to loosely wander, and this is when he does two things. First of all, he allows that time to give him some rest so that he can keep going and won't get burnt out. And secondly, this break also allows him time to subconsciously reflect on what he was just working on which leads to creative breakthroughs.

After taking a break from his work, he would get back into what it was that he was just doing, but this time he would be rested and ready to start again, and he would also have some new creative ideas and connections between what he was just working on, so even if he had previously felt like he had done everything he possibly could for a project in his initial focus block, he would be able to come right back in with some fresh new ideas.

This twenty-five-minute focus block allowed him to have a clear deadline and he would try to accomplish certain tasks in just one focus block so that he could get through things super fast by being absolutely focused while he was working to get things done much faster. This absolute focused twenty-five-minute period of time is what allowed him to finish things super fast because he wasn't distracted so he could gain a ton of momentum and get into a flow state. In fact, in that focus block, he could probably finish things that would have normally taken him a whole day because he would have fallen victim to life's distractions and he would have gone through his day reactively and wasted a lot of time because of the time it takes to transition and refocus after being distracted by doing things like responding to emails.

Francesco Cirillo created this time management technique which is known as the Pomodoro Technique. It got this name because as I mentioned, his kitchen timer that he used was shaped as a tomato, and in Latin tomato is Pomodoro.

Going back to the 80/20 principle, the most important thing is that you figure out what 20% of your inputs provide you with 80% of the results. What are the things that you spend 20% of your time doing, but those things still contribute to 80% of your overall end result? You need to figure out what this is, whether it be the product that you are selling that provides you with 80% of your total income, or the content that drives the most traffic to your site, to name a couple of examples. Once you have an idea of what this is, you also need to figure out what the flip side of this is. What is the thing that you spend most of your time on but that drives little to no actual meaningful results? This could be things like checking your email, or maybe it's the product that you have spent tons of time on creating and trying to sell it, and yet it is still only contributing to 20% of your profit. What you need to do now is figure out how to structure what you are doing to focus more on the things that actually move the needle in a meaningful way that makes it worth your time and then focus on that. Take it from 20% of your attention to 100% of your attention and quadruple your results.

Peter Drucker once said that "Nothing is less productive than to make more efficient what should not be done at all." Although it can sometimes be hard to discern, there is a HUGE difference between busywork and productivity. Anyone can be 'busy' but the question is whether or not you are actually producing meaningful *results* from what you are doing. A lot of people wear the fact that they are busy as a badge of honor, but who do you think is more successful – the man who works eighty-hours each week and makes $100,000 a year, or the one living on the beach who hacked his time and successfully mastered his productivity by only focusing on producing the things that actually matter and outsourcing or delegating the rest. This guy on the beach is only working ten hours a week, and yet he is bringing in $150,000 a year. Who is more successful? Definitely the second guy. And honestly, even if he was making let's say $50,000 a year, I would argue that he is still richer and more successful than the other guy making $100,000 because if you take into account how much they work and do the math, then you will find that the first guy is making $62.5/hour which is not bad at all, but the second guy is making $104/hour. Although the second guy would be making less money overall, I would argue that he is richer because he is making enough to live comfortably and work less, and since he is able to have the flexibility to live at the beach in let's say Costa Rica or really wherever he wants, he can convert that money to pesos, and in that economy, he will be rich.

In his book High Performance Habits, Brendon Burchard talks about figuring out what your Prolific Quality Output is and then focusing on that. In the dictionary, prolific is defined as being 'high-scoring' which is exactly what I have been talking about. You need to find the areas to focus on that have a high ROI (return on investment) in regards to the amount of time that you put in in order to gain a given result. The way to be productive and achieve greater results is by doing less and getting rid of the meaningless time wasters and tripling down on the things that bring results.

Speaking of Brendon Burchard, he said "Figuring out what you are supposed to produce and learning the priorities in the creation, quality, and frequency of that output, is one of the greatest breakthroughs you can have in your career". The way to achieve success is to stop consuming in this information age and start actually producing in a meaningful and productive way that has a positive ROI.

If you look closely at any successful person, you will notice a pattern. They started off trying to do lots of things well, but as I said earlier, you can either have widespread mediocrity or greatness in one thing. Once they realize this and cut out the 80% of things that they don't need so that they can focus especially on the 20% of things that produce the 80% of their results and then focus on that to quadruple their results, then they tend to see a turning point in their career. Every successful person reaches this point when they realize that in order to be productive, they need to cut down and narrow their vision. Steve Jobs went through this exact thing with Apple when he completely discarded several of Apple's products so that he could scale his products that were producing the best results, and in becoming more laser focused he was able to go global and change the world with his products.

Find your Prolific Quality Output and then go all in on that thing, and that is how you will scale that thing and exponentially grow towards your ultimate success. Until you get clear on what your PQO is and then get rid of the meaningless things, you will remain average and have widespread mediocrity. But once you get clear on that one thing that actually drives meaningful results and then focus on that one thing and allow it to become your entire tunnel vision focus, that is when you will scale and unlock your limitless potential with maximum productivity. The way to do more is to do less.

Archimedes was right when he said that with a lever long enough he could move the world. If you are able to work smarter rather than just working harder, then you can hack your time and achieve massive success. Some people will tell you to work harder. Others will say that you need to work smarter. I say you figure out how you can work smarter, and then work harder in that direction.

10 IF YOU ONLY FOCUS ON THE END RESULT YOU WILL LOSE

Jim Rohn said that you should "Become a millionaire not for the million dollars but for what it will make of you to achieve it". Earlier I talked about how you should set unrealistically big goals and allow those goals to motivate and drive you. The problem with these goals is that they can't be solely focused on tangible and extrinsic things, such as to simply make millions of dollars. Although this can be your goal, it shouldn't be your only focus, because something that is much more valuable than the millions of dollars is the person that you have to become to earn that.

I am sure that you have probably heard stories of people who win the lottery and after a couple of years of extravagant living they find themselves completely and utterly broke. When you become a millionaire without doing anything to earn it, you won't be able to handle it because you didn't have to work your way up to obtaining that money. If you had actually earned it, then you would have had to put in a lot of work to get there, and when you finally reach that goal you would not only achieve the materialistic goal, but you would also end up with something much greater. If and when you become a millionaire, the more valuable part to that isn't the million dollars, but rather the mindset and skill-sets that you will need to develop to get there. Self-made millionaires would have likely taken a lot of time to figure out how to accumulate their wealth, and it would have been a long process. But now that they have earned their way up, they could lose all of their money tomorrow and they could easily make it all back because in earning the million dollars they would have had to level up and become someone who was capable of doing so over and over again. The thing is though that these people would never actually lose their money unlike lottery winners, because they actually earned it and so they can handle it.

The way to be successful is to not just focus on the extrinsic outcomes but intrinsic ones as well. Most people feel like things aren't working out when they feel like they aren't getting closer to a certain goal, when in reality they are, but they just need to look in other places other than the goal that is right in front of them. If you only focus on the end result and you will only feel accomplished if you reach that specific goal, then you will fail. If you only focus on the end result then you will lose.

What you really need to focus on is who you are having to become to get there. Instead of focusing on the end result, focus on the journey. If this is the way that you look at things then nothing will be able to stop you. If you actually focus on and love the journey, then you will see setbacks and failures as temporary and as a chance to learn and grow so that you as a person will be better for the next time.

When you come at your goals from this perspective then you will be able to constantly be improving and you will become the person that you need to become to actually have earned the completion of that goal, and sure enough, once you become that person you will know exactly what to do.

You need to understand that who you are is always changing, and so you need to be consistently pushing yourself to become better than you were yesterday, and you need to move forward with a growth mindset like we talked about earlier.

The only way to be successful is to love the journey of actually putting in the work. You should genuinely love to fail and put in the work because it makes you feel fulfilled and super engaged with what you are doing. If you hate the journey, then the end result isn't worth it, and you probably won't be able to get it anyway.

The journey is more important than the outcome because it is what shapes you into your future self, and you get to decide and ultimately design who you want that to be. Your future self is shaped by your daily actions, so you need to have your actions of today match your ambitions of tomorrow.

You need to love the journey not only because of who it shapes you into, but also because the only way to be truly happy in life is to live in the moment. Although you should have your end goal in the back of your mind and it should still influence your decisions and shape your daily actions, you still need to live in the moment and be in tune with the journey in your daily life in order to be truly happy. And if you are happy and you truly love the journey, then there is no way that you won't eventually get to where you want to go.

As I said earlier, happiness isn't a by-product of success. Even though you likely see successful people who seem to have it all and they are living the dream life who happen to be happy, they are not actually happy because of their success. It's actually the other way around. They aren't happy because they are successful, but rather it is because they are happy and optimistic about the future that they are successful. If your only focus is in making it to the next mountain peak and then the one after that, you will never have time to actually live life and you will become stressed out by the stress that will overwhelm you and, in the end, you might end up achieving success, but it will be meaningless. The way to actually achieve true success is to enjoy the climb along the way, and in doing so you will be happier, and this will get you on that upward spiral towards your ultimate success.

Setting goals is important to have a clear path of what direction you need to go in, but you can't only focus on the final outcome and forget about the small details and the things that you need to get there. You should never let your big goals cause you to become obsessed with the bigger picture and forget about the important details of how to get there. When you focus solely on the end result, you lose sight of the journey to get there, and so instead of taking meaningful action, you get sucked in to excessive planning and trying to figure out how you can accomplish this big goal, and this can first of all become overwhelming, but also you need to understand that excessive planning is really just fancy procrastination and it provides you with no actual results to show for your work. If you keep on moving forward this way and don't take the time to enjoy the climb of getting there and you only focus on the mountain peak ahead of you, then you will eventually finally reach the peak, only to find yourself feeling empty inside. Although you should feel ecstatic that you finally accomplished the thing that you were after, the only thing that you really feel is a sense of emptiness deep down. You feel like you won, but it just doesn't feel right because you didn't take the time to enjoy the process of getting there. It is also scientifically proven that our perception of a future event is much greater than the actual event. This could apply to us expecting the cold water to be much worse but then once you hop in you realize it wasn't actually that bad after all, for example. Or it could also apply to what you expect to feel when you finally succeed and accomplish your goals. You think that the reward will be much greater than it actually is, and once you reach the peak you will find that the climb was really the best part, so don't spend it worrying and only focusing on getting to the peak.

You need to realize that just because you have reached the peak doesn't mean you are successful. Achieving the goals that you set for yourself doesn't actually mean that you are necessarily truly successful. A lot of people tie their feelings of self-worth to their goals, and so when they fail to accomplish those goals, they feel like a failure themselves and they don't consider the fact that that failure actually made them into more of a winner, because they were able to overcome it and grow and learn from it.

So many people anchor their existence to their goal, and so when their goal fails it drags them down with it. If you do this, you will never succeed, because along the journey towards accomplishing your goals you are going to fail. The plan will fail, but you can always have a new plan, just make sure that the end goal remains the same and don't allow your temporary setbacks to drag you down and make you lose sight of your goals. Instead of tying yourself to your goals, what you really need to do is enjoy the journey, and when the inevitable setbacks get in your way, you will no longer be dragged down with the temporary failures, but rather you will look at the distance that you have travelled to get there, and you will understand that that setback forced you to become even better for the journey ahead of you.

Whatever the end result is that you want to accomplish, it comes down to the process. If you only focus on the end result then you will lose. Let's say for example that your goal is to lose fifty pounds. This is a pretty hefty goal, and if you look at it as just the end goal then it seems too overwhelming and you don't have any idea where to even begin, and so in this situation most people simply don't. If you were to at least start though, you would eventually find yourself keeping track of your weight loss, only to feel even more overwhelmed because you will likely look at it as only five pounds lost after a couple of weeks, and you will feel discouraged because that means that you are only 10% of the way to your goal. This is when most people would get back into their negative habits and start living reactively once more. If you were to look at it from the angle of actually enjoying and using the process, however, then you would see things differently. You would then be able to see the distance that you have travelled from where you began rather than just the distance that you have left to go. This will allow you to remain motivated and keep going, which will ultimately lead to you accomplishing that goal.

You also need to proactively design the process. The only way to accomplish your big goals is to design a specific process of getting there and have a plan for the day to day that eventually leads to the accomplishment of that goal. Instead of focusing on the goal and how far away you are from it, you need to start today and engineer the positive daily habits that will work towards getting you there. When you get this process set in place, the work becomes easy because you are no longer overwhelmed. You will know exactly what to do, and when you consistently do a little bit each day you will gain momentum leading up to your goal. Instead of measuring yourself up in regards to how far you still have left to go, you will focus on the process and the journey of it all, and you will look at how far you have come, and this is what will allow you to keep on moving forward.

I think that the reason why we become hard-wired to naturally be outcome-oriented and focus on the end result is from the school system. When going through school, your only focus really is just on getting a good grade in each of the subjects, and in all honesty, you probably never really cared about what you walked away from that course with, other than the outcome of the slip of paper with your grade on it. Instead of focusing on the process and having a genuine curiosity to learn, your focus is on just figuring out what will be on the next test, making sure you know enough to pass, and then moving on to the next outcome goal. This is the worst way to achieve success, and it is important that you need to break free from this habit of being outcome-oriented and you need to learn to actually love the process and who you become to get that given result.

Christopher Nolan was a struggling director in the 1990's, and all it took was a simple shift in perspective that led to his success today in directing films such as Interstellar and Dunkirk. He said it himself "What I learned very early on, and I'm very grateful for the lesson, is that I could only be making films for the sake of making films. To only engage in telling a story for the process of telling the story, not for the gold star at the end. You have to cross into this world of just pleasing yourself, just doing something because you want to do it."

When you only focus on the end result, you create a contract with yourself to only be happy when you achieve the given result, and the problem with this is that it never leads to true happiness. When you live this way and you only focus on the end result, then you won't be happy at all during the journey. But at least once the hard work is over and you finally achieve the goal that you were after, then you will be happy, right? Wrong. As I said already, the actual event is a lot less than what you imagined it to be. You may think that when you finally achieve your biggest goal that you will then be able to finally be happy, but the truth is that after the short-term boost in dopamine goes away, then you will adapt to the level of happiness that you had before you had your success, because this is now your new reality and so you feel empty inside without anything to work towards. This type of adaptation is called hedonic adaptation, and it makes you become addicted to outcomes. Once you achieve that level of success, you adapt and that becomes your reality, so now you need an even higher dosage and so you get back to work again, and since you are outcome oriented, you aren't able to enjoy the journey, and in the end your life ends up being a constant chase with little satisfaction.

When you only focus on the end result, you will lose. You will never be truly happy, and you will forever be chasing something that you can never truly have. The way to achieve this happiness is to instead learn to love the journey. You should have your big goals and allow those to drive you, but then have your attention on the journey, and don't anchor yourself to your goals, but rather define your self-worth based on the setbacks that you are able to overcome, and the better person that you were able to become because of this. Focus on the journey and not only will you be happier, but you will also be unstoppable.

11 THE LAW OF ATTRACTION IS MEANINGLESS WITHOUT THE LAW OF ACTION

You could have so many ideas but until they go into the stage of actual execution, they suck. An idea is just an idea, and if you just keep it in the back of your mind then it is worthless. A horrible idea that someone executes on is more likely to succeed than an absolutely amazing idea with no execution. Wayne Gretzky said that "you miss 100% of the shots that you don't take". Imagine that me and LeBron James were having a free throw competition, but there was a twist – LeBron James wasn't allowed to even take the shot. Even though I suck at basketball, I could still beat LeBron James if he didn't take the shot.

The best book was never written. The best video was never published. The best idea was never executed. You will never know how great your idea could be until you try, and you need to understand that there have been so many people who have sent their idea to the grave with them quite possibly because they were worried about it failing, or maybe they thought they needed to have all of the details planned out before they could even begin. As I said earlier, excessive planning is really just fancy procrastination.

Sometimes you won't know exactly what to do, but the best way to start is to just start. If you just take that first step and actually start moving forward then you will gain momentum and figure things out along the way. If you have a couple of ideas and you are at a cross-road and you don't know what you should do, my simple advice would be to just choose one and go all in on it. Flip a coin if you have to. Let's say you were deciding between going all in on your YouTube channel idea or the business that you wanted to start, and if you started the business you will never know if you could have become a famous YouTuber, and that is what stops people from even starting. They worry about what they will miss out on if they make the wrong choice and so they wait to start anything, and years go by without them even starting. I genuinely believe that a failed business is much better than excessively planning and succumbing to procrastination. Failing at first can be good, because it forces you to level up and learn to embrace the journey, and if you have the right mindset necessary to succeed then rather than seeing the distance you still have to go to accomplish your goals, you will see how far you have come and how you have grown from your failure and learned from your mistakes.

I mentioned the quote by G. K. Chestersen earlier where he said that "done is better than perfect". I cannot explain how true this quote is. If you are a perfectionist then you will never win. If you expect your work to be perfect, then it will never get done and I believe that moving forward and taking consistent imperfect actions is much greater than excessively planning for a perfect direct route to success. Through these consistent imperfect actions, you will still be moving forward and gaining traction and momentum, and you will also be learning and growing along the way.

Gary Vaynerchuk says that "when it comes down to it, nothing trumps execution". Unless you want to become a doctor or lawyer or something like that, you don't necessarily need skill or really any idea what you are doing at first. Just start and execute on your ideas and take consistent imperfect actions in the right direction, and trust in the process and learn as you go. Experience is by far the best teacher. I don't care what type of learner you are, whether you prefer visual, verbal, physical, or whatever else, learning on the job trumps it all.

The only regrets that you will have at the end of your life won't be for the dumb things that you did or the mistakes and setbacks that you experienced along the way. Ask anyone close to the end of their life, and they will tell you that the things that they regret are the things that they didn't do, whether it be not spending enough time with their family or on their health, or not enjoying the journey, or not executing that business idea, to name a few examples. The fact that you are going to die is the single greatest motivator. If you lack motivation to execute on anything, just imagine that you were on your death bed. Do you want to be filled with regrets, or memories of the journey, the setbacks, the failures, the humility, and finally the success, and everything in between? Think to yourself if you were told that you only had a year to live, what would you do? Do that thing. Don't worry about how bad working towards your dreams might be at first, just start and let the experience shape you into who you will become.

Thomas Edison said that "Genius is one percent inspiration and ninety-nine percent perspiration". Having a great idea will only get you so far. It is the execution of that idea that you will find results from. You probably also remember the quote by Albert Einstein from when he said "It's not that I am smarter, it's just that I stick with problems longer". Even Einstein relied on the power of execution to get him to becoming the genius that we know him as. You will notice a pattern – all successful people had to work extremely hard and actually put in the work to execute towards their dreams. Sure, they could have been born with natural talent as well, but not necessarily, like in the case of Albert Einstein.

If you just take action, then you will actually be a lot farther ahead than most people who let their perfectionism lead to inaction and procrastination. Even if you have no idea what you are doing, just take the first step, and then the next, and then the next. Just one foot in front of the other. And then eventually you can look back for a second and see how far you have come, just from taking that first step, and although it didn't all go perfect or even well at all, at least you are moving forward, and in the end that is all that matters.

I hope you got a lot of value from this book, and I hope it inspired you to take action and work towards unlocking your limitless potential. Hopefully you learned a lot about things like the Law of Attraction and you can use that knowledge to use your positive intangible thoughts and ideas to attract positive experiences and realities into your life. There is no secret sauce really though. It is the thing that you knew all along, but let's be honest, you just need someone to tell you and that is what I am here to do. There is no fancy secret sauce to top off all of this information, all you need to understand is that the only thing that works is work.

Now that you have all of this information, the worst thing that you could do is put down this book and move on with your life and continue on living reactively and just going through the motions and drifting aimlessly through life. Although information is very powerful, information without application means nothing. But information plus application is when you reach a transformation.

Information + application = transformation.

You could have all of the information in the world, and some random person with no information but the ability to just take that first step will beat you. Especially in this information age, we can easily become sucked into the limitless information that is readily available, right at our fingertips. When you get too sucked into consuming this information, it doesn't allow room for you to actually produce, which is where you will actually be able to execute and get results. Since most people are so sucked into consuming all of this information, you will be at a monumental advantage if you simply decide today to stop just consuming and start actually producing and executing towards unlocking your limitless potential and crushing your goals and achieving your dreams.

In the wise words of Gobber from How to Train Your Dragon: "We believe in learning on the job". Take the challenge head on and take that first step today. Don't let this information age hold you captive. Break free and start executing and producing your own real results, and don't try to be fancy. Just take consistent, imperfect actions in a specific direction, and you will be unstoppable!

ABOUT THE AUTHOR

Teagan Adams is an entrepreneur, public speaker, and CEO. His journey began at the age of nine when he raised enough money to build a school in Kenya, Africa. This sparked his passion for doing good, which lead to his creation of Doogoods at the age of ten, a card game with a positive twist of doing good. He was on the national television show Dragons Den with this card game and has since sold his cards to families and schools around the world. He is now focusing on spreading this movement and instead of focusing on being anti-bullying, he is pro-kindness, and ending bullying will be a byproduct of raising the next generation as Upstanders instead of bystanders by making doing good fun and kindness cool. He is also on a mission to now, at the age of sixteen, end teenage apathy through empathy and entrepreneurship. He is empowering youth to take action and get more out of life. On top of all of his speaking for elementary schools, high schools and corporations, he is also launching some online programs to teach kids and teens the fundamentals of success and entrepreneurship. You can follow Teagan on IG (@teaganadams1) where you can connect with him and you will also find the motivational and value packed content that he is creating, and you can also follow his journey.

Made in the USA
Columbia, SC
19 June 2018